CONTEMPORARY ARTIST DOLLS
FROM GERMANY

by Ann Bahar and Ingeborg Riesser

Published by Hobby House Press

Grantsville, Maryland 21536

We dedicate this book to our children...

Daniel, Robert & Sonya
Sabrina & Stefan

In Appreciation...

This first English-language collector book about the contemporary artist doll movement in Germany owes much to friends and business associates on two continents. The authors - one in Pennsylvania, USA, and the other in Paris, France - worked their way through a tangle of languages to sail a straight, if unusual, course. Ingeborg Riesser interviewed each artist in German, then translated replies to questions into French before mailing them to Ann Bahar across the Atlantic in the United States. Ann wrote the English text, working directly from Inge's French-language computer sheets, then mailed drafted texts back to Inge in Paris for correction, amendment, and approval. Inge researched and wrote the history chapter and the Christa Mann artist profile. Ann translated them into English. All of this was hard work but great fun and explains why the authors' first debt of gratitude is to the German, French, and English languages and to "Franglais," in which they communicated with one another throughout the two-year span of this challenging project.

Among the people who helped this book become a reality are Regina Sandreuter, who called Ingeborg Riesser's attention to the work of Christa Mann, and Brigitte Lohrmann, a well-known gallery owner in Hamburg, who introduced us to the work of Gabriele Lipp and Ingrid Winter. We are grateful to Gabriele Lipp, who very generously mailed rare books from her personal library in Bad Oberdorf, Germany, to Ann Bahar in the United States.

Heartfelt thanks are due to the following persons for contributions that enhance the beauty as well as the collector value of this book: Andrea K. Christenson of Käthe Kruse Puppen GmbH; Kirsten Martin Stadelhofer of Denmark's LEGOLAND®; Susan Brown Nicholson, who shared delights from her Steiff postcard library; Jan Foulke, who loaned photographs of dolls by the elusive Marion Kaulitz; Mary Beth Ruddell, Margot Skelley, and Louise Fecher; Diane D. Buck, Curator of Dolls at the Wenham Museum, Inc. in Wenham, Massachusetts, who loaned photographs of Käthe Kruse dolls in the museum's collection; and Lily Bergh of Little Switzerland Dolls, who contributed outstanding photography of Brigitte Deval's "Little Girl" virtuoso piece.

Last but hardly least, the authors owe a debt of gratitude to Gary and Mary Ruddell, who recognized the need for an English-language book about contemporary doll artists from Germany and enthusiastically encouraged the writing of it!

Frontispiece: A portrait doll, Gina was modelled in 1992 and stands 33in (84cm) tall. She is dressed as a little bride and proudly wears Mother's shoes. Gina's doll and the grownup shoes provide the psychological balance between sophistication and innocence that gives this study its grace and dignity. *Photograph courtesy of Rotraut Schrott. For further information see page 124.*

Title Page: Caught in the act! "How can someone as angelic as me do *anything* naughty?" (Any experienced Mom knows the answer to that one!) *Photograph courtesy of Sylvia Natterer. For further information see page 88.*

Additional copies of this book may be purchased at $39.95 (plus postage and handling) from
HOBBY HOUSE PRESS, INC.
One Corporate Drive
Grantsville, Maryland 21536
or from your favorite bookstore or dealer.

©1995 Ann Bahar & Ingeborg Riesser

ISBN: 0-87588-430-X

Table of Contents

The prototype head, body, arms and legs for each all-wood Pongratz art doll are sculpted in clay from which a bronze master is cast. The master is then replicated, in linden or maple, on the artist's wood-carving machine. The rough-cut doll is sanded, refined, painted and assembled. *Photograph courtesy of Elisabeth Pongratz. For further information see page 98.*

The Artist Doll in Germany: An Overview

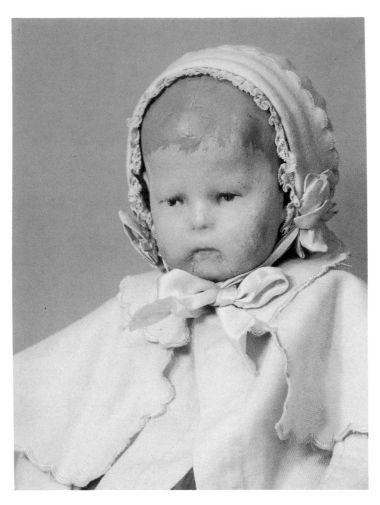

Käthe Kruse Doll #1, made from 1910. This example dates from about 1912 and stands 18in (46cm) tall. *Photograph courtesy of The Wenham Museum, Wenham, MA.*

A pair of early-twentieth-century, all-celluloid Käthe Kruse dolls, 16in (41cm) tall. The boy has glass eyes; the girl's eyes are painted. Both have human hair wigs. *Photograph courtesy of The Wenham Museum, Wenham, MA.*

For anyone familiar with the history of German toys and, most particularly, German dolls made during the "Golden Age" that began in the last years of the nineteenth century, it is hardly surprising that a new generation of gifted dollmakers is at work in Germany today. This book, the first of its kind in English, presents a select cross section of these immensely talented artists to American enthusiasts. Some, like Brigitte Deval, Hildegard Günzel, and Annette Himstedt, are international celebrities and have worked in the field for years. Others, better known until now within their native Germany, deserve wider recognition among connoisseur collectors around the world.

The modern "Künstlerpuppe" (artist dolls) had humble beginnings in the home kitchens of most of our artists. They owe their existence not to commercial or artistic ambition, but rather to a desire to create objects that resemble coveted antique dolls priced beyond the means of their admirers.

The studio role model for all these artists, in a real sense, is Käthe Kruse (1883-1968). Early in the twentieth century, she designed a simple cloth doll for her own children; the project was a conscious effort to craft a toy that would contrast dramatically with commercially manufactured dolls available at the time. Käthe Kruse wanted to create a doll type more in line with the life-style she envisioned for her own children, a life-style unencumbered by superfluous luxury. The sophisticated, costly toys of the day were, in her opinion, out of touch with the common man. That the public agreed with her became clear after a first, successful exhibit at the Hermann Tietz Department Store in Berlin in 1910.

Among the founders of the Art Doll Movement in Germany was Marion Kaulitz, for whom the sculptor Paul Vogelsänger designed prototype doll heads. Marion Kaulitz's work attracted great attention, starting in 1908, when it was displayed in Hermann Tietz's branch store in Munich. On

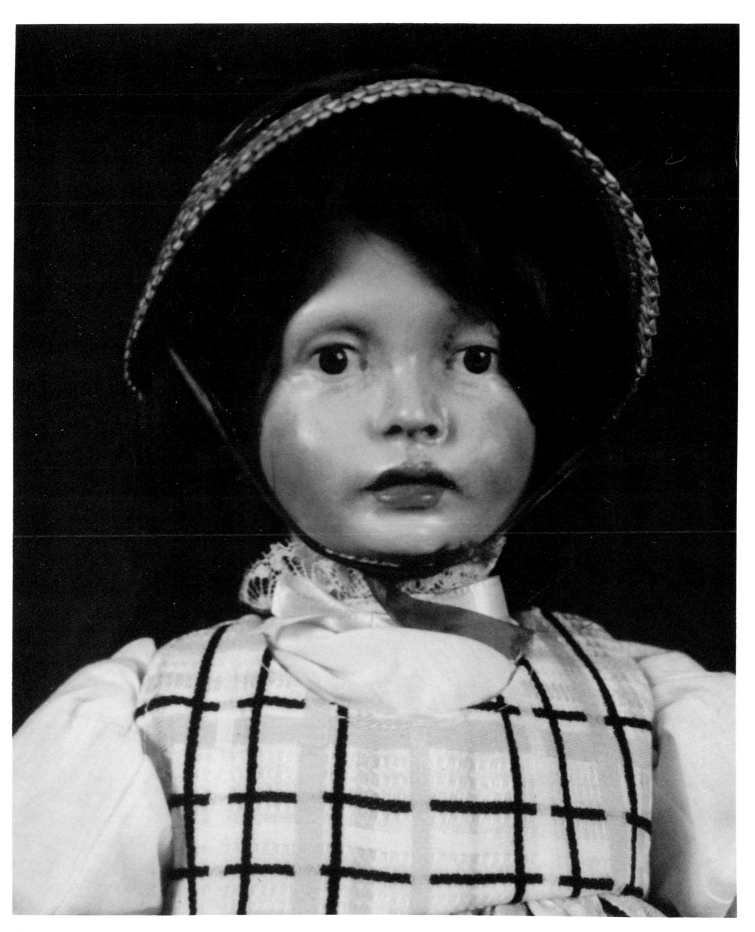

A stunning early 20th century Munich Art Doll by artist Marion Kaulitz. This rosy-cheeked, fully-jointed, all-composition child wears her original costume - no-nonsense everyday garments that sharply contrast with the frills and furbelows worn by expensive, earlier dolls. *Nancy Schwartz Blaisure Collection. Photograph by Howard Foulke. From the 7th Blue Book of Dolls & Values© by Howard & Jan Foulke. Reproduced with permission.*

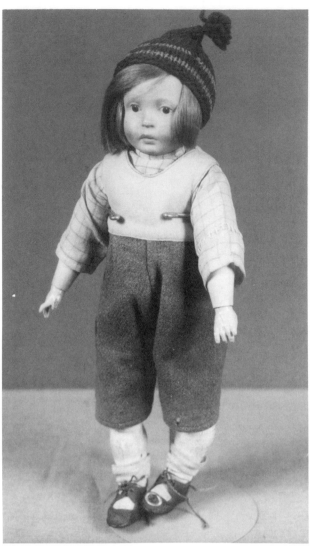

that occasion, the now familiar terms "Puppenreform" and "Künstlerpuppe" entered the literature and became subjects for debate in the world press for the first time.

The commercial firm Kämmer & Reinhardt, which had manufactured dolls since 1885 and was always quick to exploit new avenues for profit, reacted immediately to the threat of competition from new designers. To combat the newcomers, it commissioned a renowned Berlin sculptor, Arthur Lewin-Funcke, to design a head for a competitive line of dolls. Soon, Kämmer & Reinhardt was marketing its now famous "Charakterpuppen" (character dolls) whose registered trademark dates from 1909.

The important role played by Steiff in art doll history is less well known among collectors. In 1892, Steiff began to offer dolls with unbreakable heads, dressed in imitation felt. In 1902-1903, Margarete Steiff's nephew, Richard, joined the firm and the doll program was completely revamped. Richard Steiff disliked the dolls in current production. He thought them stiff, cold, unresponsive, and too much like the outmoded porcelain dolls of the day. Using felt and velvet, he created the now classic Steiff doll face and gave the dolls flexible joints so that they could be positioned in a lifelike manner. In 1910, the firm attempted to register its new dolls under the trademark "Charakterpuppe," but the request was refused, since Kämmer & Reinhardt had registered the same name only months before. Steiff used the term in its catalogs until the 1920s, however, and Kämmer & Reinhardt did not complain. If one were to establish a time line for the "Puppenreform," Steiff would almost certainly head the list, since the company's first character dolls were offered for sale as early as 1908.

Although dolls from the studios of Marion Kaulitz, Käthe Kruse, and a number of artists scarcely remembered today achieved instant fame, the public turned its back on Kämmer & Reinhardt's early character dolls. Ironically, such dolls are now collector treasures because the firm destroyed its unsold inventory and surviving examples are scarce. Collectors still talk of the incredible price realized by a K&R mold #105 at Sotheby's London auction in February 1989. A rare example of one of Kämmer & Reinhardt's earliest character dolls - a stunning 24in (61cm) girl doll with a realistic wig and side-glancing eyes - is in the Estrid Faurholt Collection at Denmark's LEGOLAND®.

Inspired by the art movement in Munich, other important firms followed Kämmer & Reinhardt's lead and retained well-known sculptors to design heads for *their* dolls. Many of these sculptors purposely concealed their identities from the public because they considered it beneath their dignity to be linked with industrial ventures. (The role played by Arthur Lewin-Funcke was only discovered in 1980!) Käthe Kruse also worked with established sculptors. Several of her early heads seem to have been designed by her husband, Max Kruse, a successful sculptor in Berlin; she also worked with the Dutch sculptor F. Duquesnois. Years later, she commissioned Igor von Jakimow to sculpt a bust of her son Friedebald who was born in 1918.

Top: A rare doll by Marion Kaulitz, who is often credited as a founder of the first German Art Doll Movement at the start of the twentieth century. This molded composition, fully-jointed boy, circa 1908-1912, marks a dramatic departure from pre-1900 stylized porcelain and bisque doll art. *Esther Schwartz Collection. Photograph by Howard Foulke. From the 7th Blue Book of Dolls & Values© by Howard & Jan Foulke. Reproduced with permission.*

Bottom: A pair of 1913 Steiff character dolls. The Dutch girl, 13in (33cm) tall, has glass eyes. The policeman (by Steiff and Schuco) wears a dark blue uniform. A clockwork mechanism enables him to march forward as well as backward. *Photograph courtesy of Skinner, Inc.*

At the start of the century, manufacturers and artists had to appeal to a double market. Dolls had to be attractive to parents (the purchasers) as well as to children (the consumers). Artist dolls crafted today are intended for adult collectors, not children, and thus creative design possibilities are infinitely greater than in the past. The modern doll artist is free to express her inner self; like canvases in a painter's studio, each of her dolls becomes an intensely personal statement by its creator.

The seeds of the current artist doll movement were planted when the Ludwig Beck Department Store in Munich devised a unique means to attract purchasers during the pre-Christmas season. In the mid-1970s, Beck filled its store with all kinds of artists whose work was offered for sale. The artists crafted their specialties in full view of delighted shoppers and were always ready to respond to questions from the public. It was at Beck's that the Munich artist Brigitte Deval-Starczewski made her first public appearance, and an article about her, published soon afterwards in the German women's magazine *Brigitte*, elicited an enthusiastic reader response. Many of Germany's leading doll artists active in the 1980s were inspired by Brigitte Deval's early work. When Brigitte Deval joined Beck's Christmas workshops for a second season, she was joined by another artist, a very young Hildegard Günzel. "I was so surprised," Brigitte confessed. "Until then, I thought I was the only art dollmaker working in Germany. There was no communications network in the 70s, no press, no way to learn of one another's existence. How times have changed!" In the years that followed, more and more artists debuted at Beck's; for many, the experience marked the start of careers that brought international recognition.

Marion Schmal, Director of the Bayrische Kunstgewerbe Verein (Bavarian Crafts Association) did much to promote interest in the new artists and their dolls. Schmal adores fine dolls and marionettes and organized annual theme exhibitions in Munich for the artists. These were rare and exciting events at which collectors could actually see the wide spectrum of doll art from many studios.

While southern Germany was being educated through the efforts of Marion Schmal and Beck's holiday workshops, far to the north the new generation of doll artists had yet another enthusiastic promoter. Hamburg gallery owner Brigitte Lohrmann, a dealer with an artist's eye, was quick to expand her collection of antique dolls to include contemporary work. She was, in fact, the first important dealer to focus on the new "Künstlerpuppen" and continues to stock a wide range of top-quality contemporary artist dolls.

Most of the early artists in the present movement are self-taught and took advantage of new techniques and newly invented, convenient materials. Their studio careers coincided with the introduction of synthetic clays like Sculpey® and Cernit®, and with the development of small, reasonably priced home kilns designed for low-firing clays. They had no need for professional moldmakers or costly, industrial-quality kilns. Only Annette Himstedt elected to work with a classic porcelain that requires high-temperature firing and elaborate

One of the Blues.

Top: A Steiff policeman, circa 1913, wears a uniform that almost matches the one worn by the immortal English constable pictured in Beatrix Potter's *A Tale of Two Bad Mice*. Steiff dressed policeman dolls for the country where they would be marketed, and it is often hard to pinpoint the police force a particular doll represents. *Postcard from the collection of Susan Brown Nicholson.*

Bottom: A pre-World War I Steiff postcard. The child wears a military officer's helmet in the Bismarck tradition and inspects troops that include three sizes of German soldier character dolls. *From the collection of Susan Brown Nicholson.*

equipment. For the others, operations (at least initially) were simple and cost-efficient, although once artists achieved success, many opted to expand their studio activities, hire additional staff, and delegate tasks that do not require "the master's hand."

In the 1990s Germany may well be reliving the "Golden Age of Dolls" that ended in the 1930s. Once again, manufacturers commission artists to design dolls for a wider market, and the resulting large editions, often in vinyl, have the advantage of being less fragile and more "child friendly" than exquisite one-of-a-kind or limited-edition studio pieces. The success of Annette Himstedt's first series of vinyl dolls was so great that a number of artists joined with manufacturers to produce vinyl dolls from their own designs. Many of these artist-designed vinyl dolls are works of art in their own right and find homes in outstanding collections.

The artist doll continues to increase in popularity in Germany. Each year, new talent swells the ranks of gifted craftspeople whose brilliant artwork wins acclaim at exhibitions and sales events, in contests, and through the media. The numbers keep increasing; the variety of images, materials, and techniques are often mind-boggling. Witness the incredible sampler of creative design and superb talent described and pictured in the pages that follow....

Above left: A trio of German character dolls manufactured between 1913-1920. At the left is 13½in (34cm) blonde Trille by Kestner. Johanne (center) is by Hertel Schwab & Co. Trunte (manufacturer unknown) has a bisque head, brown bobbed wig, and round glass eyes. *Photograph courtesy of LEGOLAND® A/S.*

Above right: A group of dolls from Kämmer & Reinhardt. The big doll at the rear is 24in (61cm) tall, with a realistic wig and side-glancing eyes. Hansi, up front, is a 1909 sailor boy with a bisque shoulder head and painted eyes. *Photograph courtesy of LEGOLAND® A/S.*

Left: The *Kaufhaus Beck* (Beck Department Store) on Munich's historic Marienplatz. Beck sponsored artist workshops to entice holiday shoppers during the 1970s and early 1980s. Many of today's top German doll artists credit Beck as the "cradle" of the contemporary artist doll movement. *Photograph courtesy of Ingeborg Riesser.*

Christiane Besch

"I really had no interest in dolls until six or seven years ago when I was looking for a hobby that would use my artistic talent and training, permit me to work at home, and, hopefully, would pay for itself," explained Christiane Besch from her studio in Königswinter. "Everywhere, one saw and read about artist dolls, so I decided to couple doll artistry with my lifelong passion for historic costume." Christiane bought a book that explained the basics of porcelain dollmaking and began what has proved to be a fascinating (and elusive) search for in-scale fabrics and trims appropriate to the various periods in western history that her dolls reflect.

This gifted lady has a two-track art background, with degrees in painting as well as textile design. She studied at the St. Martins School of Art in London and at schools of fine art in Hamburg and Aachen. Over the years, first through formal classes at art school and later through independent study, Christiane expanded and deepened her understanding of fashion history. The subject had enormous personal appeal. It offered an ever-changing kaleidoscope of texture, color, and design and opened a window onto the art, drama, and psychology that make up human history. "Historic costume has fascinated me since my student days," the artist told us en-

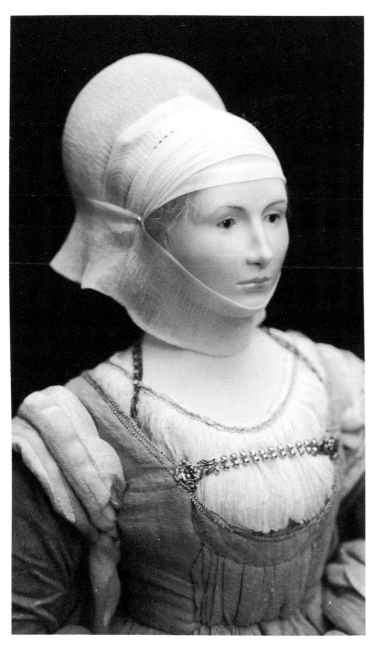

A "young lady" from Christiane's studio wears a *circa* 1528/1530 German-Swiss costume. The doll's face and headdress may be inspired by the portrait of Burgomaster Jacob Meyer's second wife, Dorothea Kannengiesser, in Holbein's magnificent painting, "The Darmstadt Madonna." *Photograph courtesy of Christiane Besch.*

The greatest challenge this artist faces is to locate in scale fabrics and trims that are true to the periods she elects to depict. Note the splendid interaction of texture and color in the gorgeous 16th century costume worn by this Besch creation. *Photograph courtesy of Christiane Besch.*

thusiastically. "The exquisite grace of Gothic gowns, the dignity of Renaissance dress, the frivolous ruffles and laces of the rococo - it's all marvelous. Each period in the history of fashion reflects an outlook peculiar to the times. Just think! For millennia, human hands have crafted this vast, varied, pageant of costume. What a struggle to transport precious velvets and silks from Italy to northern Europe, sometimes on the backs of donkeys, sometimes in the holds of sailing ships. But people did this, because from the beginning fashion has been very important. Even in the Stone Age, being well dressed involved far more than fur pelts and a club!"

Christiane sculpts the original model for each of her limited-edition porcelain doll heads from a special air-drying clay. For the prototypes for doll hands and feet she uses synthetic material that resists breakage during mold making. "The faces seem to model themselves!" the artist said. "Probably, without realizing it, I incorporate details from heads I've seen in old paintings. And sometimes I pull details - a chin, a forehead, a nose - from sketchbook records of living faces I've found interesting over the years. I prefer to sculpt mature individuals," Christiane added, 'but I keep trying to expand my range of types and ages. I love to pair old and young, grand-

parent and grandchild. Such groups call up complex emotions and memories out of one's own experience. They look back into the past and forward to the future and are very stimulating."

Porcelain components for Christiane's dolls are made according to traditional techniques. Each piece is poured, polished, fired, painted, then fired again. For adult figures, editions are limited to five to ten; child editions tend to be larger. Eyes are glass; mohair wigs are cut and styled by the artist, who rolls tiny curls with skewers or toothpicks and sets them with chemicals used for real-life permanent waves. Doll bodies are cotton calico, well stuffed and reinforced with steel wire. Finished adult dolls average 20in (50cm); children are 12in (31cm).

For this artist, the greatest challenge in each studio adventure is to locate fabrics and trims appropriate to the historic period the doll represents. Each era has its own fashion silhouette, preferred fabrics, and styles. Finding suitable yard goods for historically accurate 16th or 18th century costumes in today's marketplace is difficult indeed. Robes must hang naturally; pleats and folds must be free of ugly bulk. Cloth must be fine textured and patterns must be in scale. Christiane

Christiane's gifted hands and magic needle produce authentic portraits of every period in the history of fashion. This elegant beauty, circa 1905, is dressed to shop the Paris boulevards or to enjoy chocolate, luscious pastry, and gossip at a table in the Prater, the famous park in old Vienna. *Photograph courtesy of Christiane Besch.*

The costume worn by this elegant 20in (50cm) circa 1633 woman shows the graceful décolletage of Stuart dress. The dark gown is accented by a single strand of fine pearls and a deep fall of lace offset by a bronze silk ribbon. *Photograph courtesy of Christiane Besch.*

12

dyes, paints, and embroiders the exquisite yardage used for her doll costumes. Sometimes she overlays patterned fabric with transparent silk gauze to simulate antique brocade. Whenever possible, she uses old rather than contemporary fabrics. Lace trim is almost always antique, since she considers most modern laces too coarse for her purposes.

When Christiane Besch crafted only adult historical figures, her dolls' costumes interested her more than their faces

and "souls." But ever since she began crafting child dolls in addition to adults, her focus has shifted, a fact that surprises no one as much as the artist herself. "Now I want to deepen and expand my mastery of child doll art," she said. "And I've noticed to my surprise that the more children I sculpt, the less I fuss over the minutiae of doll costuming. The doll itself, *the child*, is becoming increasingly central to my work."

Age and youth juxtaposed add poignancy to this group, which is representative of the avenues currently being explored by the artist. The grandmother, an elderly church-going lady, circa 1860, from the cathedral town of Ulm, poses with two country children, a boy with a hoop and a little girl who holds a favorite doll. *Photograph courtesy of Christiane Besch.*

13

Brigitte Deval

"The Sandman," a dark tale of magic, love, and madness written by 19th century German romantic E.T.A. Hoffmann, fascinated Brigitte Deval as a child. "When I heard this story for the first time, I was deeply moved and attracted by the idea that a dollmaker might craft a doll so like a living human being that a young man could fall hopelessly in love with it," Brigitte told us, adding: "The idea never left me, to achieve this miracle, to create with my own hands a doll that seemed to live, to make my own 'Coppélia'."

The daughter of a well-known photographer, Brigitte Deval was born in Bavaria in 1945 and spent her childhood in Munich. Her superb gift for artistic expression made itself known early, and even today a wide range of areas within the arts continues to interest her. "I might have become a glassblower, a sculptor, a furniture designer, an interior decorator, a landscape painter," she said. "But today such directions are only dreams, since I am (quite happily) 'imprisoned' in the beautiful world of doll art."

Brigitte crafted her first doll at age six and throughout her childhood made "stock puppe," dolls built around sticks and bottles, as gifts for family friends and relatives. As part of her self-training in doll artistry, she crafted forty sets of wooden puppets, each composed of 9 to 14 elaborately carved individual figures. She crafted fantasy dolls and decorative figures, dolls dressed in exotic costumes, crèche figures,

An exquisite 22in (56cm) ballerina wears black-and-white silk gauze. A coronet of flowers reflects her peaches-and-cream complexion and complements her raven hair and intense, dark eyes. *Photograph courtesy of Brigitte Deval.*

Detail of ballerina.

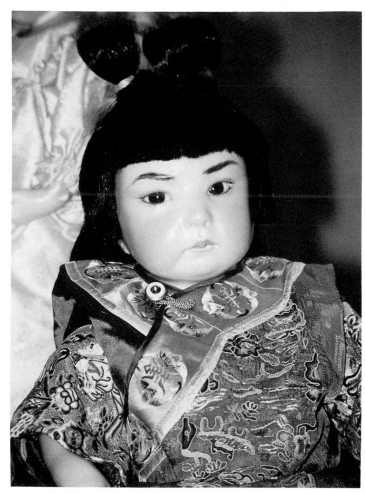

Above: The doll is seated in an old-fashioned wooden chair and wears traditional Chinese costume. Like many dolls from the artist's Siena studio, this precious 16in (41cm) Chinese child combines qualities of 19th century French and German doll art with Brigitte's own very contemporary style. *Photograph courtesy of Brigitte Deval.*

Above right: This dramatic and very tall African maiden is one of the artist's favorites among her 1992 one-of-a-kinds. Colors and fabrics were chosen to enhance the figure's regal presence. *Photograph courtesy of Brigitte Deval.*

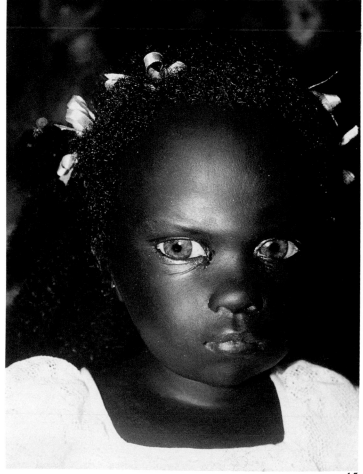

A young black child wears a square-yoked white dress and a crown of white silk hair ribbons. She gazes at us with interest and some curiosity, yet maintains the calm presence characteristic of Brigitte's dolls. *Photograph courtesy of Brigitte Deval.*

marionettes and glove puppets in the classic Guignol tradition.

It was 27 years, however, before Brigitte realized her dream to create dolls in the spirit of Hoffmann's heroine, whom American readers know better as the central character in Léo Delibes' enchanting ballet *Coppélia*. During those years, she struggled to grasp the mystery, the psychology behind appealing faces and to recreate such faces in her studio. Today, Brigitte avoids obvious facial expressions in her doll sculpture. "My dolls never laugh or cry," she told John Darcy Noble in an interview published in *Dolls* magazine in 1987. "Rather they are on the verge of expressing emotion. And it is why, as someone once said, although they have very different features, they are all uncannily alike. It is because the soul of each doll is my soul."

Brigitte Deval dolls are indeed uncanny revelations of the soul. They also delight knowledgeable collectors with their artistic perfection. The artist devoted years to experiments with porcelain, ceramics, and wax in her search for an ideal medium for her doll art. For a number of years, she worked as a sales clerk in a music shop during the day and pursued her artistic quest after hours. At last, she perfected the wax-over-ceramic technique that gives her work its timeless glow, and when the first dolls produced by this method sold easily, she left the music shop to devote herself full-time to the arts. "Wax doesn't bond with porcelain," she said. "It cracks and breaks away from the glassy base. But ceramic is porous; the wax coating adheres well and will last for centuries. The trick was to find the most absorbent white clay that wouldn't discolor or develop gray or rose spots after the wax bath."

In 1971 Brigitte moved to Italy, where she discovered Lenci and the doll art of Sasha Morgenthaler. It was an education to learn that her studio work extended a brilliant tradition of European doll art, and it was equally exciting to absorb the light, atmosphere, and centuries-old art that make Italy a mecca for art lovers. More than two decades after the artist's decision to make Italy her permanent home, dolls from her Siena studio reflect the elegance and timelessness of the remarkable country in which they are created.

They also reflect Brigitte's passion for perfection. Glass eyes for her dolls are made to her shape and color specifications by an octogenarian glassblower of human eyes with a studio in Rome. Doll costumes are crafted from antique laces and exquisite fabrics that include precious silks woven on a 17th century loom worked by a Florentine master weaver. A professional cobbler crafts shoes for Brigitte's dolls. Stockings, formerly handknit by Italian villagers, are now made to order on lace-knitting needles by a craftsperson in Romania. Doll wigs of mohair or naturally colored human hair are creations of a German wig maker. Doll hands and feet are meticulously sculpted by the artist's gifted associate, Christina Gärtner. And doll bodies sewn from fabric or leather are stuffed with kapok, a fine natural material imported for the purpose from southeast Asia or Egypt.

Dolls from this remarkable studio are limited editions or one-of-a-kinds, but even limited-edition dolls appear to be unique pieces. When interviewed for *Contemporary Doll Magazine* in 1991, the artist told writer Anna Galli that all her pieces are different. "I open the mouth a little different, or change the expression a bit...And I produce very few one-of-a-kinds. Out of 90 to 120 dolls a year only 12 to 20 are one-of-a-kind dolls."

For collectors and connoisseurs who know the artist's story, each of her dolls, with its calm face and glowing wax complexion, seems alive — the portrait of a living being with intelligence and depth of soul. One cannot help but think that Brigitte has probably come as close as one can in the real world to creating the doll of her dream, Coppélia!

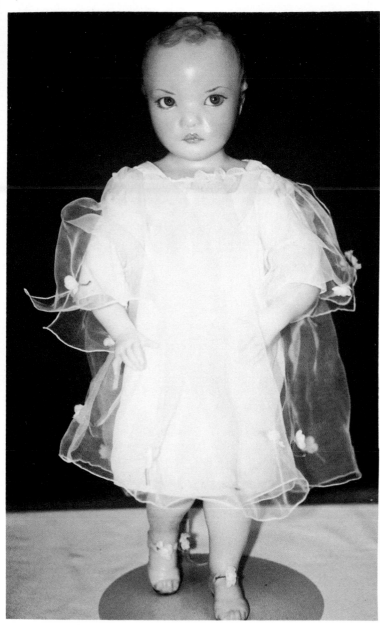

Brigitte's 18in (46cm) barefoot baby wears the most delicate of white dresses. The piece is reminiscent of 18th century Neapolitan crèche art. *Photograph courtesy of Brigitte Deval.*

A 1993 dream piece, this exquisite rendering of Hans Christian Andersen's "Little Match Girl" fuses soft textures with muted, old-world colors. Brigitte Deval is among the few contemporary artists capable of building the patina of centuries into work crafted today. *Photograph courtesy of Brigitte Deval.*

Left: Eyes for this wistful beauty, as for all Brigitte's dolls, are hand blown by a maker of human eyes in Rome. The wax-over-ceramic technique is the outgrowth of decades of experimentation and gives this artist's dolls a "skin" that radiates the warmth of living flesh. *Photograph courtesy of Brigitte Deval.*

OPPOSITE PAGE: A 1993 virtuoso piece titled "Little Girl." Here, Brigitte has crafted a "living child" surrounded by dolls in the styles of various contemporary artists. *Photograph by Pamela Setchell. Viewpoint Photography. Courtesy of Little Switzerland Dolls.*

Below left: Another 1992 beauty that echoes the Golden Age of Dolls! The wig is styled to give an impression of disorder when, in truth, every hair has been placed according to the artist's specifications. *Photograph courtesy of Brigitte Deval.*

Below right: This dreamy miss is dressed in blue silk and wears a crown of blossoms. The doll's eyes have an angled oriental cast that is accentuated by the lines of the dress. *Photograph courtesy of Brigitte Deval.*

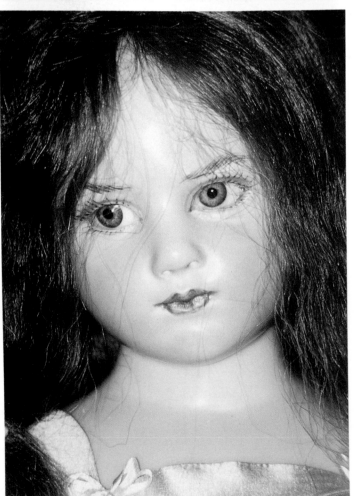

18

Verena Eising

Verena Eising's dolls have bisque heads, arms and legs, and bodies of sturdy cotton reinforced with wire armatures. This willful-looking young lady is an interesting composition in blacks, whites, and reds. *Photograph courtesy Verena Eising.*

Verena Eising was born in Nuremberg in 1955 and grew up in the picturesque lake-side resort of Starnberg, eighteen miles southeast of Munich. Verena's artistic gift manifested itself early. As a child, she loved to recreate human form and personality through art and designed her first doll, a birthday surprise for her mother, at age fourteen. While still a schoolgirl, she worked with silver, painted, sculpted, and mastered the craft of furniture restoration. By the time she had graduated from high school, she was an expert in so many areas that she found it impossible to limit herself to a single professional track.

She reacted by turning her back on studio crafts altogether and accepted a position as technical assistant at the Max Planck Institute for physics research. But Verena couldn't adjust to the regimentation and routine at the Institute and soon gave up the job. "So there I was again," the artist told us, "face to face with the seemingly unsolvable problem of my own existence. And I enrolled in a course of study in ethnology, archeology, and the history of civilization at the University of Munich.

"Then one day I was strolling in Munich and quite by accident stumbled on one of the first shops to specialize in artist dolls. I reacted as though to electroshock!" she said. "I knew instantly that *that* was what I had to make. And very soon afterwards I crafted my first dolls - clowns and characters out of my fantasy world."

It was months before the 22-year-old artist found the courage to offer those early dolls for sale, and she was delighted when her very first doll was purchased by a Munich goldsmith. "Two years later, the goldsmith's gallery was burglarized," Verena said with a grin, "and it was amusing to hear that the thieves took my doll along with everything else!"

Verena Eising's earliest dolls and marionettes were studio fantasies that echoed the shadow world of German folk legends, Greek mythology, and the often-dark undercurrents of dreams. A favorite theme was the faun, a mythological creature, half man and half beast. An enchanting faun marionette from Verena's studio is pictured in Marion Forek-Schmahl's *Kunstobjekt Puppe* (Kunstverlag Weingarten, 1990).

The artist continued to craft fantasy dolls and puppets in the years that followed her marriage and the birth of her children. But gradually, as she observed her small son and daughter grow from infancy to toddlerhood, her perspective began to change. "More and more I was attracted by the purity of their natures," she told us. "I felt the healing power of innocence and simplicity and took pleasure in their one-on-one reactions to real-world experience. Their surprise, joy, astonishment, and sorrow changed the direction of my artwork, and around 1986 I started to craft child dolls."

It took time for Verena to find the right medium for this new work. She experimented with a wide range of materials and was close to despair when the problem was solved by a friend. "My old friend Sylvia Natterer (see page 88) gave me a superb gift: lessons in how to craft plaster molds, how to work with porcelain. And several years later, in 1989, after many tears and numerous studio disasters, I finally mastered the medium and was free to develop my personal style."

Verena models the prototype for every doll head directly in clay, then refines her work with delicate tools, including surgeon's scalpels. Sculpting a new head may take anywhere from one to six months, depending on the clarity of the initial idea and problems encountered when translating the idea into clay. A mold taken from the finished sculpture is used to produce a limited series of twenty-five dolls. The first firing at 2282°F (1250°C) is followed by two more at 1382°F (750°C) to fix the porcelain colors used for delicate features and rosebud complexions. Eyes are painted, never glass.

Doll bodies are crafted from sturdy cotton, well stuffed and reinforced with steel wire armatures. Verena admits that she prefers sculpting, painting, and assembly to costume design. "It's difficult to find suitable textiles, for one thing," she explained. "I only use new, natural fiber fabrics, and I dress all my children in contemporary fashions. I design and sew all their clothing myself, but I employ professional knitters to craft the dolls' pullovers, stockings, and caps from 100% pure wool. Wigs are mohair or human hair, made to my

Shy and adorable, these wee twins with their blond mohair wigs, rosy cheeks, and handknit booties are outstanding examples of the artist's work. "There is a healing power in the innocence and simplicity of childhood," Verena said. *Photograph courtesy Verena Eising.*

The artist tells a story through the faces and body language of this enchanting twosome. The boy is bold and self-assured, with cap pushed to the back of his head and hands thrust into his trouser pockets. The little girl, by contrast, is shy and holds fast to a favorite toy, a Punchinello in the style of Verena's early work. *Photograph courtesy Verena Eising.*

This blond beauty, barefoot and dressed in becoming pastels, makes a lovely study for the camera. Observe how the doll's painted eyes avoid contact with the viewer, how child and bear are locked into a very private psychological space. *Photograph courtesy Verena Eising.*

specifications." Finished dolls range from 14in (35cm) to 18in (45cm) tall.

For this Munich-based artist dollmaking is a multilayered experience that gives satisfaction psychologically and philosophically as well as through hands-on studio work. She is fascinated by the healing power of "play," the peace of mind that comes with total focus on studio projects. "I love to craft dolls, wonderful three-dimensional images of human beings," Verena said. "Each face, each body tells a story. And since children are uninhibited in their expression of emotion, there is no end to what one can learn by observing them."

Note the exquisitely-painted features and complexion of this perky young lady dressed in her party best. *Photograph courtesy Verena Eising.*

The same girl and bear that appear on the previous page, but everything changes with the addition of a younger sibling. The psychological space swings open; what was a wistful study is transformed into a celebration of love and companionship. *Photograph courtesy Verena Eising.*

A pair of girls whose dominant personalities belie their diminutive size. "Trotzkopf" ["stubborn head"], the plump redhead shown at the right, is one of the artist's most popular collector dolls. *Photograph courtesy Verena Eising.*

Sigrid Grote

This versatile ceramicist possesses a rare gift for observation, an artist's ability to reduce observed reality to meaningful design elements, and magic hands that give three-dimensional form to her inner vision. Sigrid Grote's crowded studio in the north German city of Bremen is a busy workroom. Here the artist crafts earthenware and stoneware dishes and pots, designs plates and vases for a local porcelain factory, and, drawing on her skill as a master potter, crafts stunning contemporary dolls.

Sigrid may well have inherited her artistic gift from her remarkable grandfather, with whom she spent many joyous childhood hours. An old-world craftsman for whom play and work were synonymous, he created new toys and dolls from found objects and broken bits of nursery wreckage. Over the years, he gave hundreds of delightful, reconstructed playthings to lucky children. "My grandfather and I searched for broken bits of old toys in the street; sometimes people gave things to him," Sigrid remembered. "I watched him take the damaged toys and dolls apart and replace broken components with good ones from similar toys. One of the dolls that he gave to me contained parts from at least three other dolls, yet the proportions were excellent and she was a lovely plaything. Some-

times my grandfather salvaged bits and pieces to construct original fantasy toys conceived in his imagination. I especially loved the horses and acrobats on sticks that he carved from wood. Those acrobats performed the most outrageous tricks. He even made dollhouses, furnished and accessorized down to the last detail to provide a luxurious lifestyle for the china inhabitants. The charm of these delights was further enhanced for me because I actually saw them magicked out of the simplest objects, from things people had thrown away as rubbish."

Sigrid's own education in the arts was a haphazard affair. She worked in a shipyard; she taught youngsters in a children's home; she took courses in painting and the plastic arts; she trained in ceramics and goldsmith studios. And she taught herself through close observation during visits to museums, galleries, and art shows and through contact with other artists and craftspeople.

The artist started making dolls in her Bremen studio about thirteen years ago, after an old doll discovered at a flea market revived memories of a bittersweet experience from her own childhood. "When I was three or four," she said, "I was given a worn-out doll with a papier-mâché head and a body stuffed with straw. I loved her until suddenly she vanished. My mother had thrown my doll away because it was dirty, varnish was peeling from her face, and straw was falling out of her body. Good reasons from an adult's point of view! But I loved that doll and felt no kinship for the clean new toy I was given by way of replacement. The doll at the flea market awakened a well of deep feeling, and since then I have been intrigued by all sorts of dolls, even the Kachina dolls of the American southwest."

The artist's studio dolls are composites of children she has seen, in life or in photographs. She remembers faces, behavior patterns, what one child has said, the special way another handled its toys. The images fuse and a doll child is born within her imagination. Some are boys; most are girls.

Each limited edition of 30 begins as a sculpted clay head from which the artist derives a two-part plaster mold. Molded doll heads are made from a specially prepared composite medium that includes two types of clay and ceramic coloring. Sigrid pours liquid porcelain into the sockets for the doll's eyes, then fills the rest of the mold with the clay mixture. After a first firing at 1620°F (900°C), the rough surface is filed with emery paper. A light coat of transparent varnish is brushed onto the fixed porcelain eyes, which are

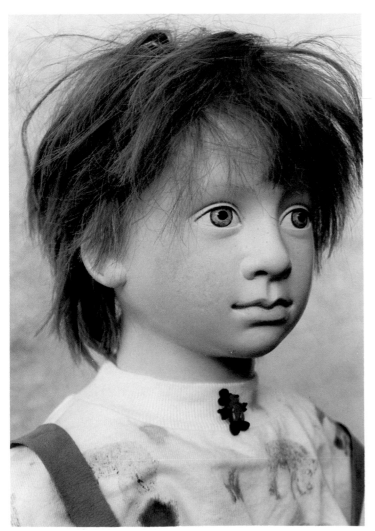

Hendrik, like all Sigrid Grote dolls, is a beautifully designed limited edition inspired by children the artist has seen and studied. "Few of my dolls are actual portraits of real children," she explained. "Rather, they are composites that incorporate facial expressions, behavior, play patterns, outfits worn by children I have observed. All this fuses to become 'new' individuals within my imagination." *Photograph courtesy of Sigrid Grote.*

Hendrik, 23in (58cm) and Sevkin, 22¹/₂in (57cm), were made in 1992. Note the exquisitely painted porcelain eyes and carefully styled human-hair wigs. *Photograph courtesy of Sigrid Grote.*

This 22in (56cm) doll was crafted in 1992. Like all Sigrid's doll costumes, Maraike's dress is intentionally simple and crafted from natural fiber fabrics. *Photograph courtesy of Sigrid Grote.*

Above left: Josephine, crafted in 1991, is a stunning 20½in (52cm) black doll whose natural-fiber fabric outfit complements her ethnic roots. The artist frequently adds painted accents to fabrics, which greatly enhances the completed works of art. *Photograph courtesy of Sigrid Grote.*

Above right: This lovely child doll, with her dreamy eyes, exotic costume and red hair ribbon, was inspired by a little girl Sigrid observed at a local flea market. When the doll was completed, the artist discovered to her surprise that it closely resembled a friend name Sevkin. *Photograph courtesy of Sigrid Grote.*

Left: Crafted in 1991, 20in (50cm) Coco has a ceramic head, hands, and feet and a cotton body stuffed with special cotton batting. *Photograph courtesy of Sigrid Grote.*

then overpainted with vitreous colors that are also used for eyebrows and lips. The finished ceramic head, hands, and feet receive a coat of wax and are attached to a cotton fabric body stuffed with special cotton batting. Because Sigrid is, before all else, a ceramicist, she likes to experiment with a variety of surface techniques for her dolls. A favorite trick is to plunge head, hands, and feet into flesh-tinted liquid slip to provide the doll with a "skin." (To protect porcelain eyes during this process, the artist coats them temporarily with latex.)

Costumes are important to Sigrid, who sews simple outfits from old and new natural-fiber fabrics. "I find some fabrics at the flea market," she explained. "Sometimes I take new clothes apart and use the cloth; sometimes I buy new yard goods. I often combine fabrics or even tint old linen dish towels and damask tablecloths when their woven patterns suit a project-in-progress. I enhance fabric texture by adding shells, feathers, beads, little figurines, contrasting threads. Sometimes I paint portions of a doll's clothing to achieve a special effect."

Sigrid Grote dolls, with their "windblown" human-hair wigs and deceptively simple stylized features, are complex works of art that are in private as well as museum collections. Sigrid's focus is ceramics rather than dollmaking *per se*; thus each new work from her studio combines the versatility and skill of a master potter with a sensitive three-dimensional portrait of childhood.

Top: Niki, 21in (54cm) tall, relaxes comfortably on a doll-size folding chair. The doll's delicate peaches-and-cream complexion contrasts dramatically with her coarse dark hair. *Photograph courtesy of Sigrid Grote.*

Bottom: Detail of Niki.

OPPOSITE PAGE: Yoko, oblivious of the camera, is a lovely study. The 21in (53cm) girl is lost in a private dream world, and the artist's choice of an abstract-patterned fabric and the seemingly random placement of the little duck pin add dimension to a remarkable mood piece. *Photograph courtesy of Sigrid Grote.*

Alice is proof that, in the hands of a master, stylized features subtract nothing from a doll's expression and the sense of life that it exudes. Note the care with which the artist has combined fabrics, colors, and selective detail to produce a beautiful composition. *Photograph courtesy of Sigrid Grote.*

Detail of Alice.

Hildegard Günzel

The artist made this gorgeous one-of-a-kind Princess in 1988. The wax-over-porcelain beauty has a wire armature skeleton. *Photograph courtesy of Hildegard Günzel.*

Dolls lent joy to Hildegard Günzel's childhood in post-World War II Germany, where the artist was born a mere two weeks after hostilities ended in 1945. "When I was two years old my family lived in one room because we lost everything in the war," she told writer Karen Bischoff during a 1991 interview for *Dolls*.

Christmas 1947 provided a memorable counterpoint to the difficulties of everyday life in the immediate postwar period. "My parents made a Christmas tree," Hildegard told *Dolls* magazine. "My mother made me one doll out of stockings.... When I came into the room and saw this, I fell down on my knees and I cried." For a child in her situation, the setting must have appeared magical. "That was the most wonderful doll I ever had in my whole life. It was the first doll I remember and I carried it with me always."

Love of dolls provides no "open sesame" to the world of dollmaking, and when Hildegard made her career choice in the arts she pursued a degree program in fashion design. She earned a masters degree at the prestigious School of Fashion Design in Munich, then embarked on a successful career in the field. At the same time, she began to amass a formidable collection of antique and contemporary fabrics that, years later, would provide a unique costume source for her one-of-a-kind and limited-edition studio dolls. Professional track and the doll world fused at last, in 1973, when Hildegard visited a friend and saw her collection of antique dolls. She was enchanted by the dolls' beauty and charm but appalled by their cost! And, as so many doll artists have done before her, she resolved that if she couldn't afford to buy beautiful dolls, she would make them herself.

Her first doll was made of plaster. Although the artist considered it a failure artistically, it opened the door to the fabulous creative potential of three-dimensional sculpture. The power of coincidence and writing contacts at German hobby-craft magazines led to an invitation to test a brand new sculpting medium, and so Hildegard had the thrill of being the first artist, worldwide, to work with Cernit®. She loved the way the new synthetic clay handled and used it in her studio until she met Mathias Wanke, a German show organizer and owner of a dollmaking supplies company, who introduced her to porcelain. After a single porcelain craft seminar, she was hooked! Today, her limited-edition and one-of-a-kind studio dolls are wax-over-porcelain, with prototypes modelled in Plastillin® rather than Cernit®.

"I model the head, shoulders, hands, and legs for each new prototype directly in Plastillin®. A plaster mold is made from the prototype, and the porcelain is poured. Studio assistants clean and smooth porcelain arms and legs," Hildegard explained, adding, "I clean each doll head personally when it comes out of the mold, using a piece of fine organdy, tulle, and a damp paintbrush. Firing is at 1220°C (2228°F), after which all porcelain components are painted with traditional oil-base porcelain paint."

All of Hildegard's studio dolls have top-of-the-line glass eyes and hand-knotted human-hair or mohair wigs. Their costumes are exquisite confections designed by the artist, who uses antique or contemporary fabrics and trims from her vast personal collection. Doll bodies are constructed over a wire armature, which allows dolls to be posed easily by collec-

tors. The artist is proud that the right hand of each of her studio dolls is positioned differently from the left hand; the right foot is positioned differently from the left foot. "This detail doubles the labor for the sculptor/dollmaker," she explained. "But it's worth it. It adds tremendous interest to the completed composition and links the doll to the dynamic of real human beings."

Hildegard Günzel's association with Mathias Wanke led to her well-known "Classic Children Collection" of large-edition vinyl dolls which were produced between 1988 and 1990. After Wanke's untimely death in 1989, the artist developed a working relationship with The Alexander Doll Company in New York City. Each year at toy fairs in New York and Nuremburg, she introduces a new limited-edition collection designed for The Alexander Doll Company. Dolls for Alexander include vinyls as well as smaller, more expensive porcelain limited editions.

Despite the pressures of designing within a tight calendar and a grueling travel and show schedule, Hildegard Günzel continues to produce about 40 one-of-a-kind, wax-over-porcelain originals in her German studio each year. "I love this work. I have total freedom when I design my one-of-a-kind studio dolls," she confided. "I know they will all find loving homes in European or American collections. Each and every one is created within my imagination; none are portraits (copies) of living models. Through this work I have the opportunity to give three-dimensional life to my private world of dreams."

Lotti, a one-of-a-kind child, wears an artist-designed costume that calls attention to her flaming hair. The 26in (66cm) doll was exhibited and sold at the Nuremburg Toy Fair in 1991. *Photograph courtesy of Hildegard Günzel.*

31

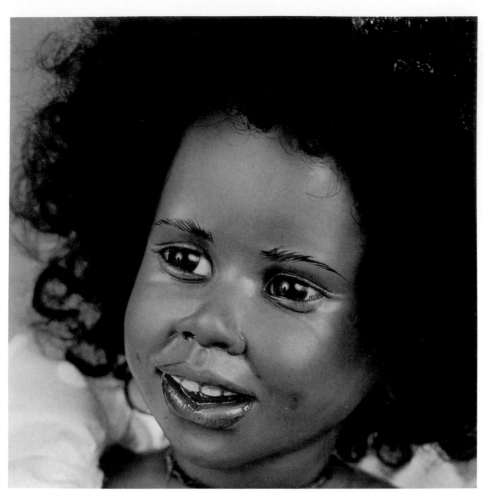

The idea for this enchanting black doll grew in the artist's imagination, then was translated into a three-dimensional sculpture in her studio. "None [of my dolls] are portraits of living models," Hildegard said. "I give three-dimensional life to my private world of dreams." *Photograph courtesy of Hildegard Günzel.*

Crafted in 1991, Birgit is another of Hildegard's superb one-of-a-kind, wax-over-porcelain children. Porcelain components are painted with traditional oil-based porcelain paint after firing at 1220°C (2228°F). Eyes are hand-blown glass; the wig is hand-knotted human hair. *Photograph courtesy of Hildegard Günzel.*

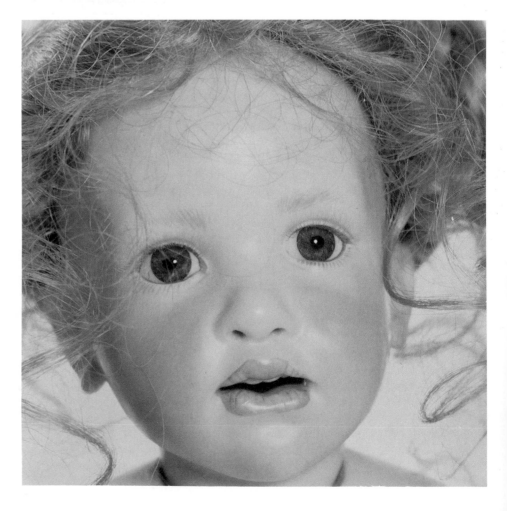

Katharina, a limited-edition studio doll, was crafted in 1992. The prototype was sculpted in Plastillin® from which the artist took a plaster mold. Hildegard explained that the right hand of each studio doll is positioned differently from the left hand, and the right foot positioned differently from the left foot. "This doubles the labor," she said, "but it's worth it." *Photograph courtesy of Hildegard Günzel.*

The limited edition, wax-over-porcelain doll was made in 1992. Although Glöckchen is unquestionably a masterpiece of contemporary dollmaking, she echoes the 19th century dolls that inspired the artist to enter the field over two decades ago. *Photograph courtesy of Hildegard Günzel.*

Bienchen, Sunshine, and Barbara, are versions of a 1992 limited edition piece. Hildegard amassed a vast collection of antique and contemporary fabrics and trims during her years as a fashion designer, and she draws on this treasure for her doll costumes. *Photograph courtesy of Hildegard Günzel.*

Rolanda Heimer

This dollmaker and sculptor, whose studio is in Biedenkopf-Wallau, is also a superb professional cartoonist, caricaturist, book illustrator, and watercolorist. Collectors familiar with Rolanda Heimer's multifaceted talents are always surprised to learn that this amazing lady was 30 years old when she registered for her first studio classes at the Art Institute in Marburg. Rolanda studied for three years at Marburg, the old university town in the heart of Germany's "fairy-tale district," and mastered the technical aspects of life drawing, portraiture, sculpture, and watercolor. "The thing I missed most at the Institute," the artist said sadly, "was the sense of fun that is vital to my personality and art - and which used to get me into so much trouble when I was a girl."

Rolanda was born in Karlsbad in 1945. Because her family lived in a remote district during her childhood, she compensated for the absence of playmates by developing a fantasy world whose inhabitants included her dolls. In school, she excelled at drawing, an art she unfortunately practiced during academic classes and all over her school notebooks. "I had a questionable reputation among my teachers and fellow students," she said. "They didn't always appreciate my caricatures!"

By the end of the three-year study program at Marburg, Rolanda's impish personality rebelled. "I felt a desperate need to create something funny," she explained. "So I made my first doll, a caricature we named Dr. Gallig (Dr. Bile). He is a cynical, grotesque 'portrait' of a retired gentleman I met in the forest collecting mineral specimens. Dr. Gallig was my first three-dimensional work of art to fuse technical precision with a humorous and very free interpretation of the subject. It's a combination I thrive on, not just as a dollmaker, but as a caricaturist and watercolorist as well. I've done a few serious portrait dolls over the years, but the experience always feels like putting on a straitjacket. I need freedom of expression in my work."

Rolanda's dolls relate directly to her passion for observation and her love of humanity. Much of the dolls' charm, along with their occasionally shocking earthiness, are due to exaggerated realism and open portrayal of the human condition, qualities which this artist reproduces to perfection. For collectors who complain that her elderly men and women, children, and life-size newborn infant dolls are rarely beautiful, the artist replies: "It's the same with real people; everyone is interesting, but true beauty is the exception rather than the rule."

For each one-of-a-kind doll, the artist rough cuts the head in Styrofoam®, then coats it thickly with Cernit®. She builds the sculptured surface by applying layers of clay over the basic form; first the forehead, then cheeks, chin, upper lip, and finally the nose. Glass eyes are inset; lids are carefully modelled and smoothed. For this delicate work, Rolanda uses the simplest of tools - a knife, a knitting needle, and a sewing needle. "Fancy equipment doesn't guarantee professional results," she told us. "Good work requires patience and meticulous attention to detail."

This artist sculpts the hands and feet for each doll as carefully as she sculpts its head. "Look at your own hands, the hands of children, of the elderly," she urges. "They are all so different and contribute so much to the personality of an individual." All sculpted components - head, hands, and feet - are fired for about an hour at 100°C (212°F). After firing, features are painted with acrylics. Bodies are cotton fabric stuffed with batting and a plastic bag filled with sand to give the finished work the weight and feel of a human infant or

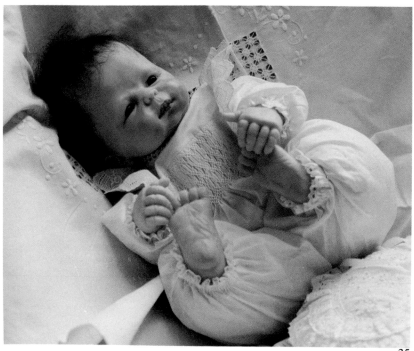

How incredible that clay, Styrofoam®, sand, and paint can mimic life so closely. This youngster isn't ready to reach for the stars; it's sufficiently challenging to reach for, and hold tight to, her own toes! *Photograph courtesy of Rolanda Heimer.*

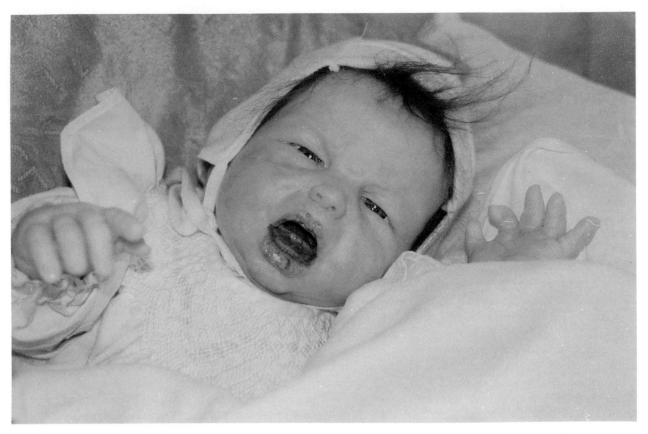

The outfits worn by Rolanda's life-size newborns are meant to "neutralize" the dolls' individuality and remind viewers that much of a baby's charm lies in its oneness with new life everywhere. *Photograph courtesy of Rolanda Heimer.*

Question: "What's nicer than one Heimer baby?"
Answer: "Heimer triplets!"
Photograph courtesy of Rolanda Heimer.

young child. Wigs are mohair or human hair, carefully styled by the artist.

For many contemporary dollmakers, costumes are an integral part of the artistic statement. Fabric, style, texture, color, accessories - all are selected with care to complement or enhance the idea that inspired the doll. Rolanda admits that although costumes for her "old people" and foreign dolls fill this expected function, outfits worn by her newborns and young children serve a different purpose. They "neutralize" the individuality of the doll, reminding the viewer that part of the child's charm lies in its shared humanity with all other children. "I create ordinary children who, by extension, are clothed in ordinary clothes," Rolanda explained. "If their outfits looked too expensive, they would detract from the overall appearance of simplicity; they would cancel the effect I strive for, that these are snapshots of everyday experience in an everyday world. The doll itself should appeal to the collector, rather than what it's wearing." Rolanda sews

some clothing for her dolls; she also commissions garments and occasionally buys ready-made baby things in department stores or specialty shops.

This artist, whose flood of caricatures, watercolors, book illustrations, and dolls have contributed much whimsy and charm to our too-solemn world, sees the future as an unfolding adventure. The evolution of ideas within her art and the chance to create new work and experiment with new directions provide constant excitement. She plans to continue making one-of-a-kind dolls ("my dolls are individuals; it would seem macabre to make them in series") and to maintain her position as an independent artist. It isn't always easy to choose between personal satisfaction with work in one's studio and public success in the large business community, she told us. "But," Rolanda said emphatically, "if I were forced to choose between them, the joy of creative experience would certainly win with me. In the end, that's what I find most fascinating - the power to give concrete form to my dreams."

While many contemporary artists give their dolls neutral, composed features, Rolanda Heimer portrays the fleeting grimace, smile, or cry that fills an instant of living time. *Photograph courtesy of Rolanda Heimer.*

Tight lips, eyes clearly planning some outrage, and a diaper squeezed tight in small fat hands sweaty with excited anticipation - all signs indicate that this baby is a bundle of mischief! The dollmaker has caught a moment that must make any mother or grandma smile. *Photograph courtesy of Rolanda Heimer.*

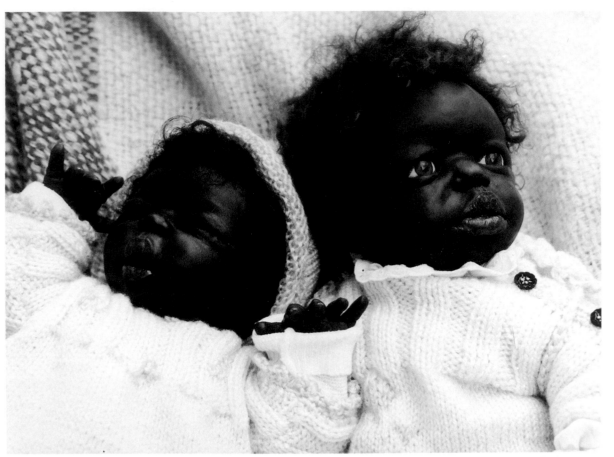

Rolanda's one-of-a-kind babies include ethnic newborns and toddlers from many backgrounds. Here, a year-old black youngster snuggles close to her snoozing newborn sister. *Photograph courtesy of Rolanda Heimer.*

The artist's old people are as intense as her brand new people dolls. Costumes are designed to give individuality to adult sculptures like this "Old Man of The Forest," in contrast to the neutralizing effect of costumes worn by the artist's baby dolls. *Photograph courtesy of Rolanda Heimer.*

Rolanda Heimer is a brilliant caricaturist as well as a brilliant dollmaker. In this cartoon, her husband, Wolfgang Heimer, scolds the young Rolanda for not making use of her artistic gifts. *Photograph by Peter Groesbeck. Courtesy of Rolanda Heimer.*

At her husband's insistence, Rolanda enrolled in a three-year arts study program, then "went professional." Have things gotten a wee bit out of hand? *Photograph by Peter Groesbeck. Courtesy of Rolanda Heimer.*

Heiri-Puppen

"A doll has the power to awaken sentiments of joy, melancholy, or sorrow in the heart of a collector," explained artists Iris Buresch and Heide Psotka. "We had the idea to awaken an independent sense of life within the doll itself, to create dolls that seemed to *feel* the emotions they communicate to the viewer."

This philosophy is the driving force behind Heiri-Puppen, the Stutensee studio that the friends established officially in 1991. Their first artist dolls debuted in 1985, however, and since that year Iris and Heide have become more and more active in the world of contemporary German doll art. Their work has won ribbons in international competitions. Starting in 1987, they organized dollmaking classes in Hamburg; two years later they were teaching sculpting in Canada. They found time to author two doll crafting books, and in the midst of this active schedule, they continued to develop their studio art. Since 1985, Iris and Heide have created a stream of delightful infant and child dolls, each of which reflects the thrust and style that typify work from this prolific studio.

By 1992, the artists had already designed more than 50 different molds for doll heads. Each is developed from an original sculpted in Plastillin®. "The molds are really just basic head shapes," the artists told us. "Size and anatomical detail vary according to the age of the child each represents, but the molds are faceless. Features and expressions are sculpted later."

Inspiration for new dolls comes from diverse sources that include live models, photographs, and recollection of individual children whose special qualities impressed themselves on the artists' memories. Once a subject has been selected, the appropriate mold is pulled from the studio shelves. Porcelain is poured, and immediately after the porcelain blank is removed from the mold, Iris and Heide sculpt features and expression into the soft, malleable medium. "This method allows us to sculpt freely without the bother of a new mold for each new doll," the artists said. "It enables us to create one-of-a-kind dolls whose faces are sculpted directly in porcelain."

Heiri-Puppen dolls are meticulously painted with porcelain colors diluted with a water-based medium. The artists pay special attention to skin tone and delicate, realistic coloring. Bodies are stuffed fabric; arms and legs are porcelain. All dolls from this studio have human-hair wigs, many of which are custom designed for particular dolls. Eyes are blown glass.

Costumes for these infants and children are sewn by a professional dressmaker according to the artists' specifications.

The rosy face and dark eyes of this little señorita are framed by a soft-textured white bonnet. Manuela, a one-of-a-kind, is 30in (75cm) tall. *Photograph courtesy of Heiri-Puppen.*

Lara is one of the elegantly sculpted porcelain busts Heiri-Puppen began offering in 1992. *Photograph courtesy of Heiri-Puppen.*

"We don't craft dolls for love of dolls but rather because through dollmaking we...express our love for children," the artists confessed. One-of-a-kind Malte, 24in (60cm) tall, typifies their porcelain children. *Photograph courtesy of Heiri-Puppen.*

Dolls from this studio have blown-glass eyes and human-hair wigs. Costumes are sewn by a professional dressmaker to the artists' specifications. This youngster is 16in (40cm) long and was crafted in 1990. *Photograph courtesy of Heiri-Puppen.*

As with their porcelain painting, Iris and Heide select styles, colors, textures, and overall costume designs that reinforce the personality and emotions of each doll.

But in the end, despite appearances, *dolls* are not the artists' primary focus. "We have a small collection of antique dolls and an even smaller collection of contemporary ones," they said. "But we aren't serious collectors. To be truthful, we don't even craft dolls for love of dolls, but rather because through dollmaking we are able to express our love for children. Each of us has two children of her own, and we cherish the memory of the intense intimacy of the child-rearing years."

"Our dolls reflect the fleeting emotions of living children," Iris and Heide told us. "Their costumes enhance the thrust of the doll and are an integral part of the design." This 18in (47cm), sleeping infant was crafted in 1991. *Photograph courtesy of Heiri-Puppen.*

Annette Himstedt

In 1978, if someone had told Annette Himstedt that she would become one of the world's top doll artists, she would have laughed. When Annette first experimented with porcelain, she didn't even know the medium was a liquid. What she *did* know was that she was driven by the artist's unstoppable urge to create.

"Even as a child I loved portrait art," she told us. "At first, I reproduced the faces I saw around me as two-dimensional images (drawings and paintings). Somewhere along the way I switched to three-dimensional modelling, which I continue to prefer today. Faces fascinate me," she added. "They reflect the personality, the soul of an individual. Children's faces are even more expressive than the faces of adults. When I sculpt a portrait, I try to reproduce the sitter's expression exactly in order to express the personality of the individual accurately. This process takes a long time when painting portraits; it takes even longer when sculpting. In the beginning I had no thought to make dolls, but as time went on that seemed the best vehicle to express what I wanted to say through my art."

This self-taught artist began working with porcelain in 1979, and during the three years that followed, perfected her command of that medium. By 1982, she was ready to go public, and a number of her early, one-of-a-kind realistic dolls were exhibited during the artist workshop at Beck's Department Store in Munich in December of that year.

The artist's interpretation of this kind of doll remained unknown to most collectors outside Germany until 1989, when she began producing porcelain dolls in limited editions of 10 to 95 pieces. Before that, she crafted six to seven one-of-a-kind dolls per year, starting with portraits of her own children, then expanding her focus to commissioned portraits of children living in and near her hometown of Paderborn, near Hamburg. Long before her work was "discovered" by the press, it caused a sensation in her local circle. Children whose "doubles" she had created were enchanted by her art, as were their families. Annette recalls the intensity of children's responses and tells with emotion of a 5-year-old girl whose porcelain portrait she crafted early in the 1980s. When the child found herself face-to-face with the finished doll, a living image of herself, she threw her arms around it and refused to let go!

In 1985, Annette wrote to author Ingeborg Riesser: "Each [of my dolls] is a unique work of art crafted in white porcelain and fired at 2642°F (1450°C). To fix the colors, 10-20 firings are needed for the head, 10-12 for the limbs, - more if there are freckles. Eyes are mouth-blown glass; wigs are handknotted and socks are handknitted. My dolls' shoes are made by a professional shoemaker and their dresses are fashioned from antique fabrics and laces."

Despite a vastly expanded atelier - in 1990, the artist opened a studio/factory at Paderborn for porcelain limited-edition doll production - the quality of Annette's art continues to dazzle collectors. It takes about a year for a porcelain limited edition to develop from an idea in her mind into a full-blown "living" doll. She sculpts the prototype directly in a special white porcelain that differs from the porcelain familiar to most of today's doll artists. Once the prototype is completed and fired (the high temperature needed for firing means a loss of 50%-60% of the work at this early stage), plaster molds are taken, liquid porcelain poured, and the greenware carefully cleaned and smoothed. Up to 60 coats of glaze are applied to create the illusion of soft, warm, living flesh in a medium as unyielding as porcelain. For her limited edition dolls, much work is delegated to highly trained assistants over whom she maintains strict control. Every evening, when her helpers have gone home and the factory is quiet, the artist works alone - modelling, experimenting, - absorbed and happy at the beloved conclusion of her 14-hour work day!

In 1986, Annette Himstedt began crafting vinyl limited editions, which elicited an enthusiastic response from deal-

Annette Himstedt's Afrika, a 1992 porcelain study, is a *tour de force* of the sculptor's craft. The carefully researched, artist-designed loincloths, necklaces, and head ornaments worn by this African boy and girl kept three employees busy for a full year at the artist's Paderborn factory. Afrika is limited to 90 pieces worldwide. The boy is 24in (62cm); the girl stands 22in (56cm). *Photograph courtesy of Annette Himstedt.*

Like many contemporary European doll artists, Annette finds Native American youngsters irresistible subjects for her sculpting. Tatanka and Sansearai, from her 1991 porcelain collection, are limited editions of 95 pieces. Tatanka is 25in (64cm), Sansearai 27in (68cm) tall. *Photograph courtesy of Annette Himstedt.*

ers and collectors at the Nuremberg Toy Fair that year. She told the authors that all her vinyl dolls are made in the production plant she established in Spain in 1986. Distributors, worldwide, buy directly from the artist, who considers her vinyl children to be as much high art, as detailed, and as exquisitely finished as their porcelain brothers and sisters from Paderborn. In fact, when author Ingeborg Riesser, a longtime European dealer/collector and doll connoisseur, looked from a porcelain prototype to its limited-edition vinyl "twin" at the 1986 Fair at Nuremberg, she found it impossible to distinguish one from the other. It took super-specialist Heinz Adler, son-in-law of Käthe Kruse, to solve the mystery. "Look at the toes," Mr. Adler advised. "The doll with more individually-sculpted detail on the toes is the porcelain model."

A series called The Barefoot Children were the first vinyl Annette Himstedt dolls available to U.S. collectors. They were followed by The World Child Collection released in 1988, and The American Heartland Collection released in 1989. The artist has continued to design new dolls in vinyl and has added babies to her offerings. Whether crafted in vinyl or porcelain, all dolls are large, detailed, and beautifully costumed in deceptively simple-looking outfits.

At the 1988 Toy Fair in Nuremberg, Annette created a sensation when she unveiled Undine, a life-size, one-of-a-kind porcelain mermaid whose staggering size was balanced by delicate detail and sensitive coloring - gray/silver hair and celadon tail and ornamentation. "I don't know why I crafted Undine," the artist confessed. "It was a challenge that became an obsession once I realized the near impossibility of the task. It took two years to complete the piece. Undine's serene expression belies the agony required to create her. The tail broke four times. Each scale on her tail was individually sculpted. There are over 1000. After that, we lost the courage to keep counting!"

As of 1992, Annette's plans include new, limited-edition vinyl and porcelain dolls. She also hopes to return to one-of-a-kind porcelain dollmaking. It will be exciting for collectors to watch her future work evolve. Undine and dolls like Lill and Jill - two 1992 porcelain child dolls with unusual coloring (Lill has lime-green hair and eyes; Jill's hair and eyes are salmon-pink!) move into a world of fantasy. At the same time, the artist's fascination with real children in the real world remains strong. The two tracks may remain distinct and separate. They may merge. Time will bring the answers.

Annette's vinyl creations for 1992/1993 included Jule, a mischievous blond youngster. She measures approximately 26in (66cm) and wears a baby-blue party dress lavishly embellished with white eyelet embroidery. *Photograph courtesy of Annette Himstedt.*

Limited edition Ling and Ming, from the artist's 1992 porcelain collection, are sensitively modelled and exquisitely costumed in traditional Chinese dress. The pair is 23in (57cm) tall. *Photograph courtesy of Annette Himstedt.*

Porcelain Tatum (1991), an edition of 95 worldwide. It is hard to believe that this introspective darling, with her dreamy eyes and wild hair, is a 27in (69cm) doll rather than a flesh-and-blood little girl. *Photograph courtesy of Annette Himstedt.*

This one-of-a-kind, life-size porcelain mermaid, Undine, caused considerable excitement at the 1988 Toy Fair in Nuremberg. Each green scale on Undine's shiny porcelain tail was individually sculpted. There are over 1000 scales, the artist said. "After that, we lost the courage to keep counting!" *See back cover for detail photo of Undine. Photograph courtesy of Annette Himstedt.*

This Swiss miss is a 1993 porcelain doll from Annette's studio. Standing 23in (57cm) tall, Nanja was introduced to collectors at the 1993 Frankfurt Toy Fair. *Photograph by Enver Hirsch. Courtesy of Annette Himstedt.*

Arana, a gypsy girl, caused excitement at the 1993 Frankfurt Toy Fair because her body, as well as head and limbs, is molded porcelain. *Photograph by Enver Hirsch. Courtesy of Annette Himstedt.*

Renate Hornung

That her dolls look like real children gladdens the heart of artist Renate Hornung, who strives to craft child dolls that appear totally natural. Proof of the artist's exceptional talent is her ability to achieve this ambition, since her dolls depict life's most ephemeral moments: a smile, a burst of laughter, a grimace, a small face raised to receive a kiss - lips pursed, eyes half-shut, rich with love, vulnerability, and beauty.

"Even as a child, drawing and painting were my great passions. Happiness was a blank sheet of paper and a handful of crayons. Unfortunately, no one encouraged me to pursue an art education," Renate told us. "It was much, much later, in fact several years after my marriage, that my talent was discovered, and my husband urged me to develop it. He bought me a box of oil paints, canvas, and an easel and I began to paint. I loved it, but oil painting wasn't completely satisfying; it wasn't quite what I was reaching for. Then, in 1984, I discovered contemporary artist dolls and knew I had found what I wanted to do. I was thrilled!"

Dolls had played a critical role during Renate's childhood. She loved them intensely and drew strength from the belief that although they were incapable of returning affection, they were just as incapable of betraying her trust. The events of one day, however, changed her feelings forever. She recalled, "To punish me for something (I have no recollection what for), my father threw my beloved doll into the kitchen stove and burned her before my very eyes. Confidence in my parents, particularly in my father, was shattered, and although I was to possess other dolls, I was always afraid to let myself love them deeply as a result of that terrible experience."

At age 34, when Renate began to develop her skill as a dollmaker, she was puzzled by her responses in the studio. "I worked like someone possessed and couldn't understand why," she said. "I felt oddly constrained, as though I was searching through the clay to find a particular image, a particular doll. Now I understand what was happening. I was groping for self-knowledge along with mastery of my craft. I

Like most work from Renate's studio, Sina depicts a significant yet fragile moment in the lives of flesh-and-blood children. Her realistic-looking mouth and teeth are varnished and she stands 33^1/$_2$in (85cm). *Photograph courtesy of Renate Hornung.*

Yasemin poses with a cuddly friend from Steiff. Note the blend of fantasy and realism in Yasemin's costume and the subtle way in which the turban is braided into the child's luxurious human hair wig. The artist pays close attention to her dolls' teeth, which she sets into the clay. Perfect teeth look unreal in a child, she insists. "The more uneven the bite, the more naturally childlike the appearance." *Photograph courtesy of Renate Hornung.*

Delightful twins Anna and Marie are 28in (70cm) tall. These darling redheads, made in 1993, are caught by the camera as they explode into laughter over a special secret. *Photograph courtesy of Renate Hornung*.

Yasemin and Desirée, completed in October 1991, each stand 33in (84cm) tall. In 1991, Renate Hornung began to sculpt the head and shoulders for each of her dolls as a single unit. "I was sick of buttoning costumes up to the chin to hide that unnatural joint," she explained. "The smooth flow of the single unit pleases me and, I believe, enhances the artistic harmony of the work of art." *Photograph courtesy of Renate Hornung*.

It's rare that an artist can fashion a perfectly harmonious work of art from such a subject! Judith, 33½in (85cm) tall, is an irrepressible miss bursting with vitality. Judith was completed in 1991. Like all Renate Hornung one-of-a-kind dolls, she has a cloth body. A steel wire threaded through the stuffed cotton torso attaches and positions the doll's sculpted Cernit® arms. *Photograph courtesy of Renate Hornung.*

was struggling to dominate the long-forgotten but powerful nightmare of my childhood doll experience. I wanted, somehow, to recreate that doll, to make it live again. And as I slowly came to terms with my own past, my contentment showed in my artwork. My early dolls were sad because I was sad. Little by little, their faces evolved, until today, with perfect harmony between my dolls and myself, my 'children' are filled with joy - and so am I."

From the beginning, Renate crafted her one-of-a-kind child dolls from Cernit® which she tinted. The head, arms and legs for each of her large dolls - they average 32-34in (80-85cm) - are individually sculpted. Every component begins with an infrastructure that is later removed to leave the doll hollow, lightweight, and easy to handle. Base material for the head is covered with Cernit®, on which the artist traces a rough outline of her idea for the face, usually a composite of her own imaginings and fleeting expressions glimpsed in magazine or newspaper photographs.

Renate cuts a slit for the mouth and develops the detail of tongue and gums, working from the exterior toward the interior. "Teeth" are purposely positioned unevenly to give a natural, youthful look. Incisions are made for eyes crafted from Cernit®, not glass. Every aspect of the head and face is carved directly into the clay; the ears are the only applied detail.

When Renate is satisfied with an evolving piece, she smooths it with her fingers, then adds eyelids. Next she sculpts the bust and attaches it to the completed head. Holes pierced in the bust enable her to sew the doll's head and shoulders to a firmly stuffed, cotton-fabric body cut from her own pattern. Steel wires, passed through the upper body, hold the arms securely in place. Fragile fingers are reinforced with fine steel wire embedded inside the clay. Before final assembly, all clay components are fired three times at 212°F (100°C) to achieve the degree of hardness Renate considers essential to her work.

This artist paints her dolls' lifelike faces with oils or acrylics. Eyes are watercolor overlaid with a coat of fine varnish. Occasionally, as with the doll Sina, Renate also varnishes the interior of a doll's mouth and its teeth. Wigs are mohair or natural human hair.

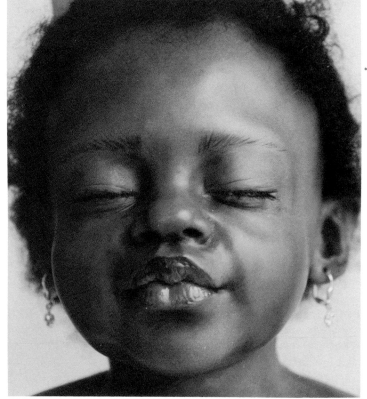

Top: Detail of Judith. A transitory expression like this one might become a grotesque caricature in the hands of a lesser artist. Instead, Judith is a huggable toothless darling, for whom life is an adventure and every day a new treat. *Photograph courtesy of Renate Hornung.*

Bottom: What a lovely dream child Bessy is! The 32in (82cm) doll, was completed in November 1990, born in the artist's imagination and inspired by a fleeting expression on the face of a little girl seen somewhere in the real world. Is Bessy asleep? Or waiting expectantly for a loving kiss? *Photograph courtesy of Renate Hornung.*

Kevin, an all-American bundle of mischief, measures 33in (84cm) tall. The artist rarely creates boy characters; she prefers to craft girls, whom she feels are more sensitive and closer to her personal psychology! *Photograph courtesy of Renate Hornung.*

Each costume is designed and sewn by the artist or carefully selected at boutiques that sell children's wear. Garments are contemporary in style, although vibrant jewelry, dramatic buttons, and bright turbans often lend an air of fantasy. The artist explained that doll and costume are meant to complement one another; together they form a complete work of art.

Since founding her dollmaking studio in 1984, Renate Hornung has experimented with a variety of techniques and has changed details in her work again and again in an endless quest for perfection. "Perhaps the most significant change in my art dolls was effected in 1991 when I stopped crafting each head and bust separately and began sculpting them as single units," she explained. "I sacrificed mobility for realism. I was sick of buttoning costumes up to the chin to hide that unnatural joint. I love my work and expect to craft dolls indefinitely," Renate told us, "but life brings change, and I am receptive to new ideas, new directions. Perhaps in a few years I'll be making something altogether different. Whatever the future holds, I know I will give it my best effort."

These lifelike youngsters, Jula and Maxi, were made in 1993. They stand 28in (70cm) tall. *Photograph courtesy of Renate Hornung.*

Tom and Denise, 28in (70cm) dolls crafted in 1993, may have had an argument but they're sure to make up. All Renate Hornung dolls are, at heart, good-natured! *Photograph courtesy of Renate Hornung.*

Jutta Kissling

Made in 1984, Jutta Kissling's first doll, Anne, is an 18in (45cm) one-of-a-kind porcelain child inspired by a turn-of-the-century photograph found in a newspaper. Like much of the artist's early work, Anne, with her straw hat, old-fashioned cotton dress and apron, and laced, black leather boots, is as much a study in nostalgia as she is a study in the psychology of childhood. *Photograph by Gerd Schwengler. Courtesy of Jutta Kissling.*

Before 1983, if someone had told Jutta Kissling she would soon rank among Germany's top contemporary doll artists, that she would give up a comfortable full-time career in business to develop a doll studio, that by the 1990s her work would be acclaimed throughout Europe and North America, she would have laughed in disbelief. "I cared little for dolls when I was a child. I preferred to read and draw," she told us. "As I grew older, I sometimes sewed or knitted outfits for my own and my friends' dolls, but that was about it. And as an adult, I had no interest in doll collecting."

She *was* interested in art and handcraft, however, and over the years she studied sketching, sculpture, pottery, and dress design. These diverse interests developed into a focus in the early 1980s when Jutta saw her first contemporary artist doll, a beautiful child from the studio of German artist Beate Schult (see page 132). "At the time, I knew nothing about modern artist dolls. To me, dolls were either museum antiques or mass-produced commercial toys," Jutta said. "That dolls existed as part of mainstream contemporary art and satisfied the aesthetic requirements of today's serious studios - this was a revelation. Since I couldn't afford to purchase Beate Schult's doll, I resolved to craft artist dolls myself."

The opportunity to do creative, original work with her hands, to create in three dimensions, and to work with fabrics, with different craft techniques, and with all sorts of materials, opened the way to an irresistible adventure. Jutta first experimented with dollmaking in 1983.

Like all beginnings, getting started was hard. "As a doll artist I am completely self-taught, and many of my early experiments ended in disaster," Jutta explained. The mold stuck to the original sculpture; badly mixed porcelain developed ugly brown spots; black magic made my kiln produce horrible shrunken dwarfs. It was 90% determination and 10% talent that kept me going! Gradually, problems receded and I gained control of my craft."

Jutta's first success came in 1984 with the creation of a one-of-a-kind doll she named Anne, which was inspired by a turn-of-the-century photograph published in a local newspaper. "The photo showed a small girl about 6 years old, wearing a hat many sizes too big for her," the artist said. "She looked directly at the viewer; her expression was rebellious; she stood with her legs apart, and she wore black laced-up boots and a white pinafore over a simple dark dress. She was the antithesis of the sugary dolls I had known, and I resolved to create a modern doll in this child's image."

Anne became a delightful study of childhood at the moment when baby softness has just disappeared and the first signs of independence and defined personality make themselves known. And, like many of Jutta's early dolls, Anne was imbued with old-fashioned, wistful nostalgia, a quality the artist has filtered out of her work in recent years. Her goal is to reveal the essence of childhood at a critical turning point; to simplify, to strip away extraneous detail and fuss to reveal the pure essence of the "essential child" between the ages of 6-10. Every detail — hairdo, painted features, costume (Jutta makes all her patterns and does most of the sewing), and choice of colors, fabrics, textures, and accessories - contributes to the artist's purpose. "It's a wonderful age, the precursor of adolescence," she told us. "It is the moment when personality, budding independence, [and] rebellion all begin to come forward. This makes an ideal challenge for the artist."

Elli (1989), 18in (45cm) tall, is one of an edition of 15 - the limit Jutta sets for all her series. The all-porcelain doll is an exquisite study of the fragile moment between innocence and knowledge. Note the way Elli's human-hair wig frames her face and enhances its delicacy. Eyes, as with every Jutta Kissling doll, are painted. *Photograph by Gerd Schwengler. Courtesy of Jutta Kissling.*

Jona (left) and Iris (right), each 22in (55cm) tall, exchange secrets in the deep woodland! This duo is so subtly composed that it's easy to miss the interplay of light and dark tones that heighten the dramatic impact. As always, costumes are designed by the artist to complement - through color, texture, design, and carefully selected accessories - the "message" she is trying to convey. Jona and Iris were crafted in 1990. *Photograph by Gerd Schwengler. Courtesy of Jutta Kissling.*

Jutta is not a portrait artist. Inspiration comes from a burgeoning collection of photographs, postcards, newspaper clips, and snapshots of friends' children. A new sculpture for a limited edition of 15 (Jutta only crafts one-of-a-kind work for major exhibitions) is modelled in Cernit® and may take three to four weeks to complete. Although the artist used to make her own molds, time constraints have forced her to assign that task to a specialist.

Unlike many contemporary artist dolls, Jutta Kissling's "children" are crafted entirely in porcelain. "I prefer to create the whole doll in one material," the Munich-based artist explained. "The body, head, arms, and legs are all made of tinted porcelain bisque assembled the classic way, with elastic and hooks. I try to achieve as much mobility as possible without resorting to ball joints or other joints that detract from the overall effect of the work of art. So it becomes critical that the body and limbs be sculpted in such a way that the assembled doll can be posed like a living child - standing dolls with arms flexed to hold a doll or flowers, seated dolls often with the trunk supported by arms behind the back."

When components emerge from the mold and have dried for one to two days, Jutta polishes them (spending four to five hours on each doll), then fires them in a special kiln with sensitive digital controls. Features are applied with water-based porcelain paints and fired two to three times. The artist paints her dolls' eyes and likes the softer, more harmonious look this gives to the finished head. Wigs are natural human hair or mohair that is dampened, cut, then styled with a hairdryer by the artist.

For costumes, Jutta prefers new natural fibers like cotton, silk, and rayon. She experiments with small samples of likely cloth; if her original pattern succeeds, she purchases fabric to complete the edition of 15 dolls. "I'm always tempted to add lace and frills to their outfits," she confided. "But I hold back. In the end, simplicity of design suits my dolls best, as it suits me in my personal life. I stay with black and white fabrics as much as possible and keep accessories, detail, and fuss to an absolute minimum. The accessories I do add are selected with great care and are major factors in my artistic statement."

Since 1985, Jutta Kissling has exhibited a new collection of approximately 12 dolls in editions limited to 15 at the Nuremberg Toy Fair every year. Her work has appeared in leading contemporary artist doll exhibits throughout Germany and France, and one of her dolls, Ania, was purchased by the Musée des Arts Décoratifs in Paris in 1990.

Top: Vera's vivacious personality is evident in the angle of her head and her laughing mouth, and echoed by her wine-red knitted pullover, white beret, and deep-auburn hair. More and more, the artist strives to depict the basic truths of childhood, subtracting nonessential details. Vera is 22in (55cm) tall and was made in 1989. *Photograph by Gerd Schwengler. Courtesy of Jutta Kissling.*

Bottom: Ania, 22in (55cm) tall and made in 1990, demonstrates how successfully the artist strips away extraneous detail to reveal the soul of a child. Ania's velvet dress is a simple pattern made up in black-and-white. Her face is framed by thick dark hair and a white frilly collar. There is artistic tension in her seated position; leaning slightly backward with weight resting on the hands. This piece was purchased by the Musée des Arts Décoratifs in Paris. *Photograph by Gerd Schwengler. Courtesy of Jutta Kissling.*

Sandra (1990), with her black-and-white silk dress and lace collar, appears less mature than many Jutta Kissling children. Mama dresses Sandra well, but the youngster still prefers play to vanity - note the beloved doll, the rumpled dress, the sliding socks. The patent-leather sandals, like all shoes worn by Jutta's dolls, are handcrafted by the artist. Sandra is 22in (55cm) tall. *Photograph by Gerd Schwengler. Courtesy of Jutta Kissling.*

To see the artist's progress over the years, observe the difference between 22in (55cm) Norine, made in 1991 and 1984's Anne. Norine sits with hands behind her back, legs relaxed. The utter simplicity of her dress sets off the extraordinary richness of the sable fabric from which it is made. Feet and hands are stylized. The beautifully styled human-hair wig, red cheeks, and intense painted eyes add drama to this artistic statement. *Photograph by Gerd Schwengler. Courtesy of Jutta Kissling.*

Using her favorite blacks and whites, Jutta Kissling has created a perfect composition. Matou, 22in (55cm) tall, echoes the impish beauty of the young Leslie Caron. The bright accent of the ball, the vibrant red of the felt hat brim, and the tension built into Matou's pose provide clues to the psychology of this irrepressible miss. *Photograph by Gerd Schwengler. Courtesy of Jutta Kissling.*

Bottom left: This one-of-a-kind piece was made for a 1991 exhibition, "Fetish Dolls," held in Munich. A striking abstract study, it measures 24in (60cm) high. The head is mounted on a plaster post ornamented with pearls, strips of leather, and dried herbs. The arm is porcelain; hair is red mohair. *Photograph by Gerd Schwengler. Courtesy of Jutta Kissling.*

Bottom right: Note how the hair of this 1993, all-porcelain creation is styled to contribute to the viewer's understanding of the child's personality. Named Marieke, this doll is 20in (50cm) tall. *Photograph by Gerd Schwengler. Courtesy of Jutta Kissling.*

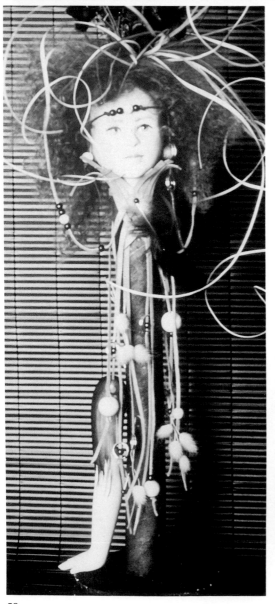

Leonie (left) and Linni (right) are a direct, no-frills statement in black and white accented with subtle, carefully selected accessories. The all porce- lain dolls were made in 1993 and are 20in (50cm) tall. *Photograph by Gerd Schwengler. Courtesy of Jutta Kissling.*

Maria Luise Lehner-von Lemcke

Maria Luise Lehner-von Lemcke, an avid reader, enjoys sculpting dolls that depict favorite characters from fiction and fable. "The dollmaker has power to give visible, palpable form to legendary heroes and heroines, as well as to beloved characters out of juvenile fiction," confided the artist. "To interpret these personalities, to bring them to life, is a source of great joy for any artist who loves books as much as I do."

This explains the presence here of characters like George Bernard Shaw's Covent Garden flower seller, a youthful Eliza Doolittle, as well as an utterly adorable Goldilocks clutching (of course!) the littlest bear. The artist's Little Prince, a three-dimensional embodiment of the child that has endeared Antoine de Saint-Exupéry's fable to generations of readers, is another example of Maria Luise's talent. The Little Prince stands against a curtain of stars, his black-booted feet firmly planted on Asteroid B-612 where, as monarch, he rids his planet of baobabs, tends a rose, and sweeps out three volcanoes daily.

Less familiar to American collectors, perhaps, is Sterntaler, a tale of a heroine from the Brothers Grimm. Sterntaler (the name means "Star Money") is an orphan whose sole possessions are the clothes on her back and a loaf of bread. As she wanders through a wintry countryside, she gives her possessions away, one by one, to fellow travelers whose plight is even more desperate than her own. In *More Tales from Grimm* (New York, Coward-McCann, Inc., 1947), translator/artist Wanda Gág tells how "as the girl was going through a forest, there came still another child who said she was cold and begged for something to keep her warm. The girl [Sterntaler] hardly knew what to do, for she herself had nothing left but her undershirt.

"'Still,' she thought, 'it is so dark that no one can see me,' so she gave her undershirt to the child, and then stood there bare and shivering in the cold. Oh, what should she do now?

"The answer came from above, for suddenly something came falling out of the heavens — a shower of shiny stars which, on the way down, turned into silver dollars, hundreds and hundreds of them. And something else happened too, for although but a moment before, the girl had given away her last little garment, she now found herself wearing a new one, made of the finest linen. Into this she joyfully gathered up the silver dollars, and was rich all the days of her life." The artist's Sterntaler is portrayed in her fine linen garment, at the moment when the star shower is magically transformed into coins. This ceramic limited edition of 25, crafted in 1991, combines the imaginary world of the poet with the artist's power to give form and substance to a world of dreams.

This remarkable artist, born in Pomerania in 1942, has fond memories of her own childhood dolls. "My three sisters and I sewed and knitted wardrobes for our 'children'. In the garden, we constructed homes for them out of stones and branches. We prepared doll feasts from berries and other small fruits. Our fantasy knew no limits..." Maria Luise's home was filled with talent and creativity. Her father was a Professor of Art; her mother wrote and illustrated children's books. Craftwork was second nature in such a household and later, after her marriage, the artist sewed and knitted for her daughters' dolls as enthusiastically as she had done for her own, years earlier. It was not until 1979, when Maria Luise and her husband adopted a ten-month-old baby boy afflicted with Down's Syndrome, that the artist began crafting dolls.

Ronia, heroine of the Astrid Lindgren juvenile classic, *Ronia, the Robber's Daughter*, sits with her friend Birk, son of a rival robber king. With them are three "rumphobs," part of the curious population of Ronia's beloved forest. One-of-a-kind Ronia was crafted in 1991, Birk in 1992. *Photograph courtesy of Maria Luise Lehner-von Lemcke.*

Sterntaler (Star Money) is the artist's interpretation of the beloved character from the Brothers Grimm fairytale. The child, having shared her last chunk of bread and warm garment with travelers even poorer than herself, is rewarded with a shower of magic coins from heaven. *Photograph courtesy of Maria Luise Lehner-von Lemcke.*

Above left: The porcelain figure of Antoine de Saint-Exupéry's Little Prince stands 11in (27cm) tall and has painted eyes. One of an edition of 25, the adorable young ruler of Asteroid B-612 sports a charming blond mohair wig crafted by the artist. *Photograph courtesy of Maria Luise Lehner-von Lemcke.*

Above right: Shining Star, a 13in (32cm) one-of-a-kind Native American doll, wears an authentic fringed leather tunic enhanced with elaborate beading. "When the head, arms and legs for a new doll are completed, I arrange them on my studio table to determine precise proportions for the cloth body," the artist explained. *Photograph courtesy of Maria Luise Lehner-von Lemcke.*

Left: Manoel, a one-of-a-kind 12in (30cm) Peruvian boy, and his furry pet llama. The artist never sculpts directly from living models, but she studies bone structure, coloring and authentic costume detail to insure that her ethnic Third World dolls are totally realistic. *Photograph courtesy of Maria Luise Lehner-von Lemcke.*

The 16in (42cm) Eliza Doolittle from "My Fair Lady" is sculpted in the artist's favorite air-drying synthetic clay, DAS-PRONTO®. Note the floral pattern of the dress fabric which transforms this youthful one-of-a-kind character into a *living* flower girl! *Photograph courtesy of Maria Luise Lehner-von Lemcke.*

Crafted in 1991, the 13in (32cm) limited edition ceramic Goldilocks hugs a favorite bear. Observe how the soft dotted fabric is echoed in the wallpaper pattern, the girl's sunburst mohair wig, and the subtle way the artist establishes psychological distance by placing the dark wood chair between the child and viewer. *Photograph courtesy of Maria Luise Lehner-von Lemcke.*

The years that followed were filled with hard work and extended therapy for her adopted son. To balance the stress of family life, Maria Luise crafted her dolls, first in cloth for the local kindergarten, later in air-drying clay. It followed naturally that heroes and heroines of stories she read aloud to her son became subjects for her doll artistry. Recent projects include one-of-a-kind renderings of Ronia and Birk, the robber kings' children from prize-winning Swedish author Astrid Lindgren's 1981 juvenile classic, *Ronia, The Robber's Daughter*. "I read the book to our son," the artist explained, "and was inspired by the lively descriptive text and wonderful illustrations."

Maria Luise's interpretation of Ronia began as a styrofoam ball wrapped round with air-drying clay. When the initial mass had dried, she inserted handblown flat glass eyes, then built up and carved the surface to transform it into the image of a living child. There is no kiln in this studio, so Ronia's poured ceramic arms and legs are oven fired in the artist's home kitchen. (For some one-of-a-kind dolls, the artist sculpts limbs directly in FIMO®.) Once components are shaped and air dried, the artist begins the laborious process of sanding and smoothing the face, refining delicate details, - the ears, nose, lips, the expressive lines of upper and lower eyelids. The completed head receives a final polishing with a silk stocking.

The artist paints her dolls' faces with DEKA-ZIERMATT®, — three coats of flesh tone, sensitive lips, fine eyelashes and eyebrows, and rose blush cheeks. Texture and styling of Ronia's mohair wig echo the duality of her forest life, with

Two interpretations of Jutta, a porcelain limited edition doll that started life as an identical molded porcelain head. *Photograph courtesy of Maria Luise Lehner-von Lemcke.*

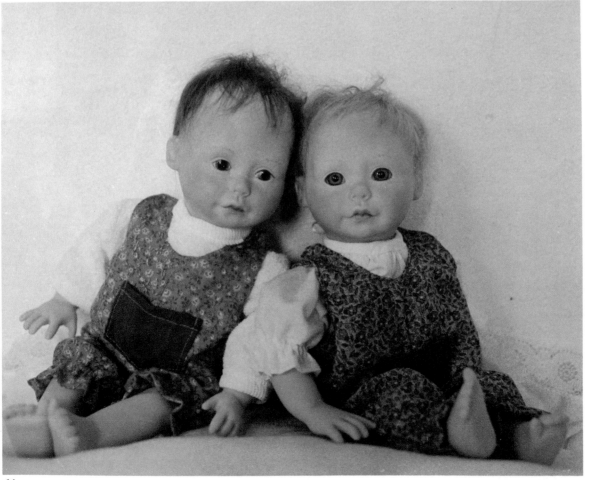

Brunette Nicki, with his painted eyes, is yet another example of Maria Luise's ability to craft highly-individual dolls within a single edition. Nicki's fair-haired playmate's eyes are hand-blown glass. *Photograph courtesy of Maria Luise Lehner-von Lemcke.*

One-of-a-kind Mia, 9in (23cm) tall, enjoys a blissful summer meadowland with friend Winnie-the-Pooh. *Photograph courtesy of Maria Luise Lehner-von Lemcke.*

its rough exterior and fragile poetic core. Costumes for Ronia and Birk are designed directly from descriptions in Lindgren's novel, and the trio of "rumphobs" (forest dwarfs) were a whimsical afterthought to complete the mood piece.

Whether a doll from this studio is inspired by a literary work or just evolves in the magic hands of the artist, it is invariably a sensitive, compelling work of art that suggests the complex psychology of a living child. Maria Luise, however, favors her storybook dolls, "I love to read and to craft dolls that derive from legends and fairytales. My adopted son and I have shared much joyous experience through our reading and the studio work that often grows out of it."

Little Hans in The Blueberry Wood, a doll based on an early-20th-century fairytale by Carsten Brandt. Hans is transformed into a Tom Thumb-sized boy and experiences wonderful adventures with the King of the Blueberry Wood and his tiny subjects. *Photograph courtesy of Maria Luise Lehner-von Lemcke.*

Elisabeth Lindner

"My work is rooted in emotion," artist Elisabeth Lindner told author Ann Bahar in an 1991 interview for *Doll Reader®* magazine. "I'm fascinated by human beings, particularly children," she continued, "and I can't describe the joy I experience each time I model a living face out of a piece of clay, then add details that make the face an individual with real feelings and responses."

This remarkable lady has been crafting dolls since 1985, although the decision to become a professional doll artist was in fact made two years earlier. "I was expecting a baby and had a lot of free time," she told one of the authors in 1990. "I saw many expensive [antique] dolls and in 1985 I started to try reproducing them." Elisabeth is completely self-taught; she mastered the rudiments of her craft through perseverance and trial and error and today ranks high among the leading artists at work in Germany. She has won several prizes in competitions and was the focus of a major exhibition at the Galerie Calico in Essen during 1989. Another one-woman show in Germany, set for late 1992 or early 1993, was in the planning stages when we interviewed Elisabeth.

Each Lindner limited-edition child doll begins life as a lump of raw clay. Every subject is an individual with its own "soul", insists the artist, who is fascinated by the infinite variety of features and expressions among human beings and, particularly, among children.

For each of her limited editions of 25, Elisabeth sculpts the head and shoulderplate, hands and feet. When the clay prototype for an edition is complete and every detail is in place, the artist crafts molds from plaster, then casts components from white china. Nostrils and mouth may be open or shut, depending on the mood and message the piece is meant to convey. Eyes are glass. Features and life-like flesh tones are painted with meticulous attention and remarkable skill. In fact, since her first tentative experiments as a dollmaker and china painter nearly a decade ago, Elisabeth Lindner has lived with an *idée fixe* about the way she wants to use color on china. "I will not reveal my method," she told the authors, "but only recently, at last, have I been able to make colors work as I have longed to see them."

Doll wigs are human hair whenever possible, and haircuts are intentionally styled to look "realistically untidy." The artist designs her dolls' costumes herself, but as interest in her work has increased, she has begun to employ studio assistants to manage the actual sewing and accessorizing. Lindner dolls average 24in (61cm) tall. A few are 30in (76cm) and occasional limited-edition "tinies" measure 13in (33cm). Once in a great while, the artist crafts a special, huge doll like Fortuna (see illustration), a 43in (1m,10cm) giantess.

The variety of child types this artist can produce is impressive, and whether she works from a living model or a photograph, her dolls do indeed appear to have "souls". Little people from Elisabeth's busy studio range from a charming Pu Yi, lost in a wistful and very private dream world, to mischievous, wide-awake Nandi, and glamorous adolescents like Fortuna. When we expressed astonishment at this broad canvas of human types, the artist was surprised. "Every person is different from every other person," she said. "So of course each of my dolls is different from the others."

Pummelchen and his best friend. This 24in (60cm) boy doll, made in 1991/1992, is a fine example of Elisabeth Lindner's art. The child who began as a lump of clay has the apparent depth and sensitivity of a living being. Pummelchen's embrace radiates genuine affection! *Photograph courtesy of Elisabeth Lindner.*

Portrait study of the artist's daughter, Janina. Sensitive modelling and remarkable control of painted surfaces are typical of Elisabeth Lindner's art.

"I will not reveal my method, but only recently, at last, have I been able to make the colors work as I have longed to see them." *Photograph courtesy Elisabeth Lindner.*

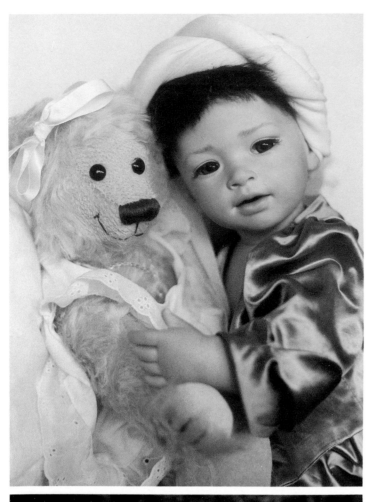

A charming Oriental boy with appealing dark eyes, turban, and bold green satin trousers and matching jacket gives an enthusiastic "bear hug" to a western friend! *Photograph courtesy of Elisabeth Lindner.*

This wee lad, a variant on the beloved Pu Yi theme, is a study in color, design, movement, and soul. *Photograph by F. an Haack. Courtesy of Elisabeth Lindner.*

This small girl, crafted in 1991, is one of the last dolls to be given painted lower lashes. Recent dolls have real eyelashes on upper and lower eyelids. The doll measures approximately 29in (75cm) tall. *Photograph courtesy of Elisabeth Lindner.*

Jessica, 24in (60cm) tall, is a plump, auburn-haired youngster in a charming blue-and-white dress with a coordinated fabric hat. The artist designs outfits for all her dolls; sewing and accessorizing are handled by studio assistants. *Photograph courtesy of Elisabeth Lindner.*

This prototype for a limited-edition doll has a human-hair wig as do most of the artist's dolls. Elisabeth intentionally cuts and styles them to look "realistically untidy." *Photograph courtesy of Elisabeth Lindner.*

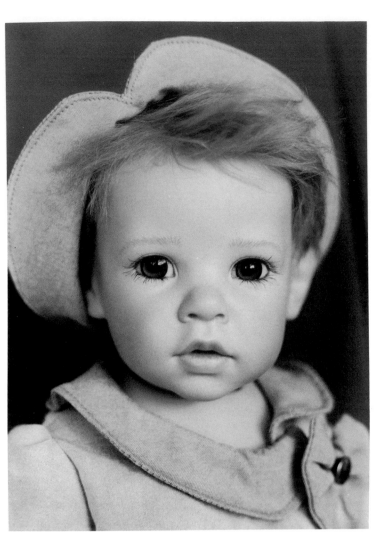

Danny's soft, full cheeks, parted lips, and silky baby hair form a moving counterpoint to his wide-awake alert expression. The 21in (54cm) doll is one of a 1991/1992 limited edition of 25. *Photograph courtesy of Elisabeth Lindner.*

The artist's first collection of vinyl dolls, manufactured by GÖTZ, was made available to collectors in 1993. The girl and boy, Pummelchen and Nandolo, stand 21in (52cm) tall, while Baby Danielle measures 14in (35cm). Nandolo sports a synthetic wig; the girls' wigs are mohair. *Photograph courtesy of Elisabeth Lindner.*

Gabriele Lipp

"I'm not a complicated person and I have no complicated aesthetic purpose," explained artist Gabriele Lipp, whose delightful needlesculptures echo cloth children from the Austrian studio of dollmaker Elli Riehl (1902-1977). Like the earlier artist, Gabriele has spent a lifetime in Tyrolean villages where, through doll artistry, she gives tangible form to a private world of ideas and dreams. "My dolls spring straight from my heart and gain life through my hands," the artist said.

From early childhood, Gabriele's talent and love for the arts was evident. Throughout her primary school years a favorite activity was drawing (she was later to work briefly as a professional designer); through middle school in her native village, she was quick to master every handcraft skill offered in the very craft-oriented German curriculum of the day. At the age of 12, the young artist crafted her first doll, to commemorate the 800th anniversary of the founding of her village. "But I never *played* with dolls when I was young," Gabriele confided. "I was a tomboy and much preferred my collection of Steiff animals. They went to bed with me for years."

In the years that followed - as a young woman, as a bride, as a busy mother of three - Gabriele continued to experiment with a wide range of crafts. She learned the art of painting on silk, of reverse-painting on glass, of pottery, and she continued to develop her gift for drawing. An older friend made

"Since childhood I have been interested in Native Americans," the artist told us, "and like all my work, they are painted with acrylics. I pay particular attention to the eyes, with the all-important dots of light that give them life." *Photograph courtesy of Gabriele Lipp.*

Few babies are more charming than Gabriele Lipp's wee papoose pictured here. The infant is tightly swaddled in carefully-researched beaded suede and reflects a lifetime love of children and Native American culture. *Photograph courtesy of Gabriele Lipp.*

This extraordinary group of needle-sculpted children from around the world includes a Tyrolean duo, a mischievous Latin American village boy and a chubby Oriental toddler. A Native American girl embraces the sleepy papoose pictured earlier, and a rosy Eskimo hugs a needlesculpted puppy. *Photograph courtesy of Gabriele Lipp.*

Listen carefully! You can almost hear the cheerful music played by the old organgrinder and his small friend with the harmonica. Gabriele's moodpiece echoes delightful needlesculpted groups crafted decades ago by Austrian artist Elli Riehl. *Photograph courtesy of Gabriele Lipp.*

sorcerer dolls and shared her craft secrets with Gabriele, who used them to create small hunters, Alpine climber dolls, and crèche figures. "But I disliked the way the children's faces looked; the craft process I was using didn't give the results I wanted. And then," Gabriele said excitedly, "I stumbled on a book, *Kleines Puppenbuch* (The Little Book of Dolls), which described the work of Austrian dollmaker Elli Riehl. It told how she used needle and thread to transform flat cloth into three-dimensional forms. I studied her methods and began experiments that continued for years."

Today, Gabriele Lipp creates one-of-a-kind cloth dolls that are coveted by knowledgeable collectors across Europe. Each doll begins as a wire armature (see diagram) wrapped around with cotton batting fastened securely with bands of fine sewing thread. The artist builds surfaces to form the doll's arms and stomach, thighs, calves, hips and buttocks. Over this "flesh wrapped skeleton," Gabriele pulls a "skin" made of fine cotton tricot tubing. Careful needlework and precisely-adjusted stitch tension provide the details of body shape. Fingers, toes, knees, and elbows are delineated; big toes and thumbs are made separately, then stitched into place.

"The head is crafted from a ball of cotton overlaid with the same cotton tricot fabric," the artist explained. "Each face is literally sculpted with stitches. I pull the thread tight to carve deep wells. With a needle, I ease stitch tension to form shallow valleys. It takes great patience and many hours of hard labor and concentration to build a face, with its eyes, nose, mouth, and all the lines and creases that show character and emotion. When I finish, the back of the head has been pulled flat, so I must add a second unit to round out the shape. I needlesculpt and attach ears and, when the work is done at last, I spray it with a fixative to prevent deformation over time."

Gabriele dampens the fabric face, then uses acrylics to paint her dolls' features. She pays particular attention to the eyes, which receive layer after layer of delicate color. The "spot of light" that awakens the eyes and gives them life is an especially crucial painting area. Doll wigs are mohair, styled by the artist.

Gabriele is as careful about designing costumes for her dolls as she is about needlesculpting their bodies. She favors old fabrics with soft, faded colors. "For my children's clothes, I arrange colors and patterns so they *don't* coordinate," she said. "I remember how it was during my own childhood as a little village girl in the years following the war." Gabriele knits her dolls' jackets and socks herself, then searches for suitable accessories in flea markets and local shops. Occasionally, her husband crafts an in-scale piece of furniture or a wooden toy for her dolls to hold.

The artist needlesculpts babies, adults and animals in addition to her favorite subjects, 4 and 5 year old children. "That's the age when faces are particularly open and expressive and give great opportunity to the artist," she explained. Gabriele's dolls are amazingly expressive for their diminutive size. Babies average 7in (17cm), adults 12in (31cm). Child dolls are 9-10in (22-24cm) tall and animals are, understandably, sized to fit the people grouped with them.

"My output will always be limited," the artist told us, "because I shall always work alone. I can't tell you how it happens, but I actually *see* each doll, complete, in my mind's eye before I begin to craft it. I plan to continue making cloth dolls. They may be less valuable in the marketplace than porcelain beauties, but they are more rare and the work gives me great satisfaction."

The authentic costume of the young Lapplander, with its cheerful embroidered trim and colorful knitted leggings, complements the youngster's sparkling personality and *joie de vivre*. The reindeer was also crafted by the artist. *Photograph courtesy of Gabriele Lipp.*

73

Gabriele's Latin-American waifs tug at our heartstrings. The impulse is to reach into the picture, to give all we can to assist this tragic third-world child and her tiny brother. *Photograph courtesy of Gabriele Lipp.*

Detail of an 8in (20cm) doll, crafted in 1993 from Gabriele Lipp's Tyrolean studio. *Photograph courtesy of Gabriele Lipp.*

An irresistible pair, these Eskimo youngsters are aglow with personality as they pose for the photographer in their warm fur parkas, faces framed by delightful sunshine ruffs. *Photograph courtesy of Gabriele Lipp.*

Carin Lossnitzer

It was preordained that Carin Lossnitzer become a doll artist. Art is in her blood! Her grandfather was a talented sculptor; her childhood home overflowed with her parents' impressive art collections. And from infancy, Carin has adored dolls. "My love of dolls began in the cradle," she told the authors. "We have family photos that show me as a tiny child with a doll in my arms. By the time I was 7, I already possessed 21 dolls."

When the time came to select a profession, Carin enrolled in a degree program at the Adolf Lette School of textile and fashion design in Berlin. Circumstances led to a 15-year career restoring dolls for museums and private collectors, a field in which, like her original doll art, she is completely self-taught. Carin has never stopped loving exquisite 19th-century dolls which are the focus of the museum she established at Coburg, but the day came when the stylized faces and fixed stares of even the finest 19th-century "bébé" ceased to satisfy her own artistic thrust. "I began to find their expressionless faces and empty stares disturbing," she told us. "I longed to create a very different kind of doll that would say what I wanted it to say. The work that followed was certainly influenced by the presence in the house of my own young children."

Today, Carin Lossnitzer ranks high among the top artists at work in Germany. Her prize-winning dolls appear in leading American and European collections. Since 1988, her dolls have become accessible to middle-range collectors through a partnership with GÖTZ®. The artist designed 16 prototypes which the firm has issued, in editions of 1000, as adorable vinyl toddlers and infants.

Carin is perhaps best known for her Sabberbabys (drooling babies), which she first crafted in 1982, and for her charming Asiatic children, third-world youngsters from the mountainous region encompassed by Thailand's "Golden Triangle." The artist is fascinated by the faces, fabrics, and customs of the East and has immersed herself in Thai culture. "I've studied their customs, costumes, and everyday tools. I've collected local dress and lengths of cloth, jewels, and accessories." In fact, the artist's empathy and knowledge regarding Thai culture make it possible for her to develop Thai child dolls as naturally as she develops dolls that represent her native Europe.

Sabberbabys evolve in the artist's imagination. Some represent children Carin has seen in photographs, but most are composites, dream infants that grow from a lifetime of observation and love of young life. Like Carin's other dolls, Sabberbabys designed a decade ago tend to be smaller than those she crafts today. Early dolls averaged 16-20in (40-50cm); dolls of the 1990s are often 27-30in (68-75cm) tall.

Head, arms and legs for each one-of-a-kind child doll Carin creates in her studio at Coburg, Germany, are sculpted directly in Cernit®. The head is built around a Styropor® core; arms and legs are complete to shoulder and thigh. The artist takes great pains with skin tone and mixes various hues of Cernit® to achieve the precise shade she desires for a particular doll. Glass eyes are inset, wigs are human hair or mohair. For her Thai babies, Carin designs special wigs which are made to order from her specifications. Doll bodies are sturdy fabric stuffed with granules, which add weight and the "feel of life" to the completed piece.

After the clay has been fired, the artist paints features with acrylics or water-base paint. Head, arms and legs are tied to the cloth torso and the doll is at last ready to be costumed. "The doll's personality and clothing form a unity," Carin told the authors. "I search for suitable fabrics at home and abroad, at fairs and in the shops. Sometimes I ask travelers to bring third-world fabrics back to Germany for me. I use antique and contemporary crafted cloth and trimmings," she added. "And I design and sew all my dolls' clothes myself."

"Clothing and child are components of a single composition," the artist explained. Carin achieves this goal with her European children like Natalie, a 20in (50cm) sleeping Sabberbaby, as well as with her tiny Asiatic youngsters. *Photograph courtesy of Carin Lossnitzer.*

Twin girls, one-of-a-kind Sabberbabys (drooling babies) from Carin Lossnitzer's Coburg studio. This pair, hand sculpted from Cernit® in 1984, measures 16in (40cm). These baby dolls, with their hand-crocheted bonnets and bibs, provided inspiration for other contemporary dollmakers during the '80s. *Photograph courtesy of Carin Lossnitzer.*

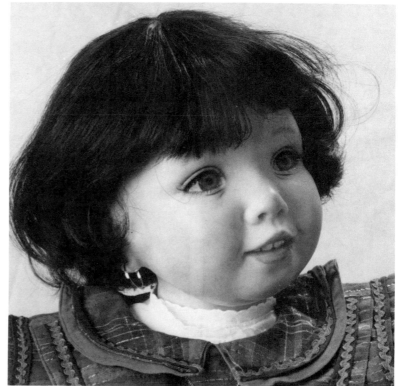

An alert, wide-awake child whose hairdo, dark-lashed eyes, and bold-patterned dress create an upbeat mood. The 30in (75cm) hand-sculpted doll was crafted from Cernit® in 1991. *Photograph courtesy of Carin Lossnitzer.*

77

The fair hair of the 27in (68cm) hand-sculpted sailor girl, provides a dynamic counterpoint to her bold navy-and-white outfit trimmed with gold braid and appliquéed stars. *Photograph courtesy of Carin Lossnitzer.*

Carin's 30in (75cm) hand-sculpted black toddler was made in 1991. The artist builds her one-of-a-kind Cernit® doll heads around a core made of Styropor®. *Photograph courtesy of Carin Lossnitzer.*

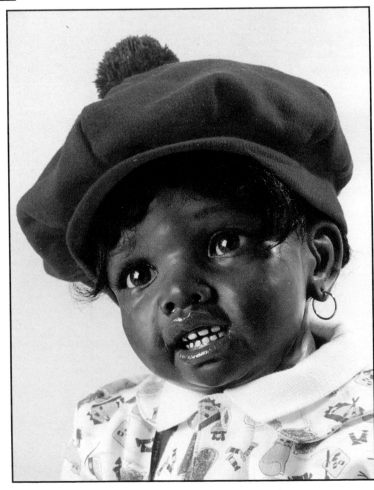

What an adorable duo! A pair of 30in (75cm) youngsters crafted in 1991. The group has a dramatic edge. The older child, less innocent than her young sibling, observes the photographer warily and holds tight to the baby's chubby hand. *Photograph courtesy of Carin Lossnitzer.*

Detail of previous illustration. *Photograph courtesy of Carin Lossnitzer.*

The 28in (70cm) sailor boy and girl dolls wear the bold navy-and-white fabrics the artist favors. Notice how, once again, Carin makes the viewer aware of the relative immaturity of the younger child. The artist mixes Cernit® of various hues to obtain the precise flesh tone needed for each of her handsculpted child dolls. *Photograph courtesy of Carin Lossnitzer.*

My Fong and Yamada are two 21in (54cm) vinyl dolls manufactured by GÖTZ® from prototypes designed by the artist. Carin's Thai children are as familiar to collectors as are her Sabberbabys. The artist spent years studying Thai culture, traditional costumes and everyday life. Today, she is equally comfortable crafting Asiatic and European youngsters. *Photograph by HP-Fotostudio. Gerd Heinlein. Courtesy of Carin Lossnitzer.*

Carin's 24in (60cm) toddler is about to burst into howls of grief. This handsculpted piece crafted in 1992 is titled *Ich will mit* which means, as every mother knows only too well, "I want to come with you!" *Photograph courtesy of Carin Lossnitzer.*

In this version of *Ich will mit*, the baby, dressed in a warm pink jacket with black pompoms, seems to have come out the victor in the age-old battle to accompany Mama! *Photograph courtesy of Carin Lossnitzer.*

Christa Mann

The work of Christa Mann evokes the fantasy world of fairies and elves, dwarfs and anthropomorphized insect and animal forms; it gives three-dimensional life to the innumerable fairy tales that play a key role in the lives of German children.

Christa, who was born in Munich, loved to listen as her father recounted the marvelous old stories that gave fire to his children's imaginations. Sadly, the tragedy of war, the early death of her beloved father, and the family's relocation in Sonneberg, obscured these precious memories which were to resurface 45 years later as major components of Christa's doll art.

Christa Mann grew up in Sonneberg, the historic Thuringian town which, before 1939, had been the hub of toy production in the western world. After the Iron Curtain divided Germany, Sonneberg continued to foster old-style cottage industry; the town produced doll wigs, plaster molds and many other items. As a youngster, Christa was fascinated by

Rubli (Little Carrot Top) is a 16in (40cm) one-of-a-kind piece. Rubli's head is soft sculpted. The entire doll is constructed from felt and cotton fabrics. *Photograph by Saturia Linke. Courtesy of Christa Mann.*

Rubli seen from the rear! *Photograph by Saturia Linke. Courtesy of Christa Mann.*

All felt 20in (52cm) Betty Blue is a one-of-a-kind doll. Betty holds two tiny dolls, one a Pierrot, the other a "little fool" from the artist's beloved fairytale world. *Photograph by Saturia Linke. Courtesy of Christa Mann.*

A delightful duet, - Little Flame and Water Droplet. Little Flame's face is spotted with soot. *Photograph by Saturia Linke. Courtesy of Christa Mann.*

Regentrude's Baby, a one-of-a-kind papier-mâché and felt piece 12in (30cm) wide, was inspired by Theodore Storm's book, *Regentrude. Photograph by Saturia Linke. Courtesy of Christa Mann.*

Little Thumbkin, a 6in (14cm) doll, asleep in a leaf. Head, arms and legs are papier-mâché; painted surfaces are wax coated. *Photograph by Saturia Linke. Courtesy of Christa Mann.*

Two of the "Five Peas in A Pod," a three-dimensional interpretation of the beloved Hans Christian Andersen fairytale. Dolls are felt and papier-mâché. *Photograph by Saturia Linke. Courtesy of Christa Mann.*

the many workshops along her daily route to and from public school. It was in the houses of these craftspeople that she first saw molds used to produce *papier-mâché* components. She watched women sew superb dolls' clothes and, with roughened housewife hands, form exquisite, tiny silk roses to ornament the toes of elegant doll shoes. At the time, Christa didn't realize how deeply she was affected by the dollmakers' world nor how profoundly it intermeshed with the beloved storybook fantasies of elves, dwarfs, and fairytale castles. It was in the spirit of these old Sonneberg family workshops that she designed her first dolls, a series she called "Chick Peas," in the style of traditional jointed dolls of Thuringia.

The forest that surrounded the family's Sonneberg home was the childhood playground for the young Christa Mann and her little sister. Toys were improvised from mosses, ferns, grasses, mushrooms, and berries. Memories of these beloved playthings were later reworked in the mature artist's imagination. During her childhood, Christa also spent long hours at the famed Sonneberg Toy Museum, and she still recalls an elderly spinning-lady doll that winked at her, a fabulous Frog queen and two wonderful early Lencis, which may have inspired her life-long love affair with felt. Among the images preserved from those long-ago days is a peculiarly clear recollection of Frau Feldkeller, a gifted artist who crafted superb gnomes from fabric scraps and whose dolls appeared, to Christa, to be alive, to have souls.

As an adult, Christa Mann worked first as a window-dresser, a professional career track that taught her much about the decorative role of dolls in art. She learned to sculpt figurines and dolls, to work with textiles and clothing accessories. After the birth of her daughter, she turned this professional training into a delightful hobby and, just as her father had done when she was a child, she crafted toys and dolls for her own little girl.

The hobby, in turn, opened new professional opportunities when, at age 27, Christa's artistic gifts were discovered and she began an apprenticeship in the studio of a well-known sculptor. She plunged into the world of sculpting, mold-making and delicate crafting of wax models. But the studio routine proved suffocating; it denied her any creative outlet. And it was then, to satisfy her personal creative instincts, that she began to craft period dolls she calls "Ladies of Burgundy," - slim, slightly arrogant, yet appealing gentlewomen that remain her favorite theme to this day.

Once the artist has worked out details for a new doll in her imagination, she sculpts a prototype that brings the small being to life. Then she crafts plaster molds and casts papier-mâché components, mixing the papier-mâché according to her own secret recipe. Molds are used 20-30 times, then destroyed. Once cast pieces are dry, the tedious sanding process begins; eyes and features are painted with watercolors or gouache, then coated with a protective wax coating. We asked why she works with papier-mâché, a medium many artists find awkward and messy. "It's a warm material," Christa replied. "It makes you want to touch and handle it. I enjoy working with felt for the same reason."

Christa crafts doll clothes from natural fiber fabrics, sometimes new cloth, sometimes old. Wigs are mohair or long-fiber plush. Wigs, shoes and costumes are crafted from start to finish by the artist herself.

From 1988-1990, Christa lived in West Germany where she worked as a designer for GÖTZ. In 1992, she exhibited her original work for the first time at a doll show. "It took great courage to step out as an independent artist," she confessed, "but I was lucky. At that show, the firm Wanke of Limburg was impressed by my work and contracted to reproduce and distribute 12 of my papier-mâché and felt designs." Since May 1993, Christa has also developed a series for the firm Reiner Martin of Sonneberg. The artist now lives in Berlin, but she delights in her regular trips to confer with Reiner Martin in Sonneberg, the town where she spent her childhood and first experienced the joys of dollmaking.

"It's impossible to explain *why* I create dolls," Christa Mann confided. "There is some unfathomable inner drive and I just keep making them." Collectors who have only recently discovered the unique work from this Berlin studio can expect many changes over the years as Christa continues to develop and refine her art. However, her focus, - dolls inspired by the storybook fantasies of a childhood lived in Sonneberg - and her preference for *papier-mâché* and felt for her charming creations will probably remain unchanged.

Kunigunde, one of the artist's Ladies of Bourgogne dolls stands 24in (60cm) tall. The doll is molded from papier-mâché; painted surfaces are overcoated with wax. *Photograph by Pierre Abboud. Courtesy of Christa Mann.*

Three dolls with heads, busts and limbs of papier-mâché. Painted surfaces are wax-coated and clothes are linen or felt. Dolls pictured average 11in (27cm) tall and are manufactured and distributed by the firm Wanke GmbH in Limburg, Germany. *Photograph by Saturia Linke. Courtesy of Christa Mann.*

A close look at one of the dolls developed for Reiner Martin of Sonneberg. *Photograph by Saturia Linke. Courtesy of Christa Mann.*

A pair of dolls from the recent series designed for the firm Reiner Martin of Sonneberg. Dolls and clothes are felt. Each mask face and bust is backed with papier-mâché to stiffen and stabilize the form. Christa Mann designed five different 18in (47cm) prototype models for the series. *Photograph by Saturia Linke. Courtesy of Christa Mann.*

Sylvia Natterer

Sylvia Natterer has always loved to work with her hands. "I taught myself to knit when I was four, simply by watching my mother knitting," she smiled. "And yes, I had dolls when I was a child, but their construction interested me more than their play value." As an adult, Sylvia put her busy hands to work and became a weaver. Her gift for designing and crafting stunning abstract wall hangings was appreciated by German architects, decorators, and private collectors who commissioned work by the artist for major hotels and contemporary high-rise office buildings. These pieces, often a staggering 12.9 yards (12m) high, were woven from sisal and wool on a giant loom and were meant to complement and enhance architectural interiors.

The artist's transformation from weaver to dollmaker began in Switzerland in the late 1960s, after she accepted a post in the arts-and-crafts department of a Swiss elementary school. As an ambitious group project in 1971, she created a marionette theatre, working first with her 8-12 year-old pupils and later with adult student teachers enrolled in degree programs in art education. "We wrote outrageous scripts, modelled original marionettes in wood composition, designed costumes from a vast range of fabrics and accessories, and incorporated every conceivable stage effect into our productions," she told author Ann Bahar during a 1990 interview for *Doll Reader*® magazine. "The theatre delighted the public and was great fun for all of us."

When Sylvia's family relocated in Munich, she put her art and marionette background to work to help restore Munich's "Kleines Spiel," one of the first of the avant garde adult puppet theatres to be relicensed in post-war Germany. "I was an active member of the troupe," the artist told us in 1990. "Whenever my baby daughter took a nap, I hurried over to the 'Kleines Spiel' to restore the wonderful old marionettes. I researched and repaired their costumes, too, remaking the princess's dress, repainting the can-can dancer's stockings. In fact, I did so much they nicknamed me the *puppenfee* (doll fairy)."

This serious, energetic and gifted artist plunged into dollmaking in 1976, the year her toddler daughter was joined by a new brother. "To help my daughter accept the presence of a small rival, I gave her a gift made entirely by myself, - a doll."

Sylvia's first doll project was an exercise in disaster! She sculpted the doll's head in wood composition. Then, impatient to see the finished piece, she painted it fast, before it was thoroughly dry. She stitched the body from stockinette fabric, stuffed it with lambswool and handed the finished gift to her little daughter. "I knew so little about the right and wrong way to do things then," she confessed. "I didn't even know I had to apply a coat of protective varnish to the painted surface," she said during the *Doll Reader*® interview. "So when my daughter hugged and kissed her new treasure and the paint came off all over her face and clothing, I repainted the features and this time I did varnish them. Imagine my horror when, two weeks later, the doll burst out in some sort of manic plague! Its face was covered with horrible bluish spots and the varnish peeled off in sheets. It seems I had done the most unprofessional thing possible; I had applied the sealant before the wood composition had completely dried. Moisture was trapped inside the head, and the thing was a ghastly

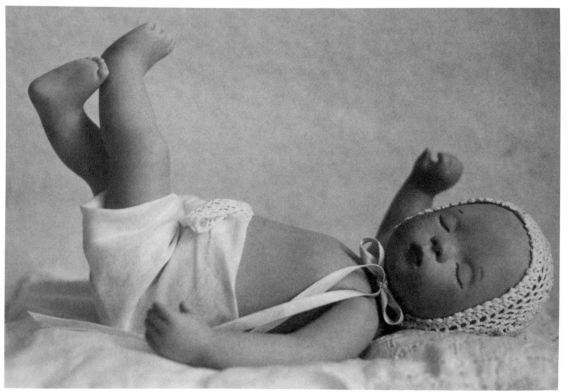

One of the artist's favorite babies, this sleepyhead is totally relaxed in a safe dreamworld of loving arms and warm milk! The baby is 13in (32cm) long and a fine example of Sylvia's power to "say more with less." *Photograph courtesy of Sylvia Natterer.*

Sylvia often groups her dolls, in this case a 11in (28cm) Tyrolean toddler enjoying a snowy outing with her 22in (55cm) big sister. The Natterers have spent years in Switzerland and the German Tyrol and love the fierce beauty of winter in the mountains. *Photograph courtesy of Sylvia Natterer.*

A perky 18in (46cm) youngster from Sylvia Natterer's Munich studio. The exquisitely-painted complexion, eyes and features are framed by the braided crown and delicate curls. *Photograph courtesy of Sylvia Natterer.*

"I want my dolls to look like dolls, not humans in disguise," the artist told us. Like Sasha Morgenthaler, Sylvia simplifies the human face and form without detracting from its living quality. The doll pictured is 19in (48cm) tall. *Photograph courtesy of Sylvia Natterer.*

Brother and sister? Young sweethearts? This charming twosome poses with a pair of feathered friends in a park setting. *Photograph courtesy of Sylvia Natterer.*

A solemn 21in (52cm) Indian girl, wears an iridescent silk sari over a patterned teal blue choli. *Photograph courtesy of Sylvia Natterer.*

mess of mildews and molds." All Sylvia could do was to trash the entire project and begin again. She learned much from that first, awful experience, but at the time it was very discouraging.

After this bumpy initiation into the complexities of contemporary dollmaking, Sylvia Natterer was determined to master her new craft from the ground up. Today, she is highly ranked in Europe's outstanding doll artist community. Each of her dolls, whether it is a one-of-a-kind masterpiece, a limited-edition porcelain baby or a comparatively-inexpensive vinyl toy for children to handle and play with, reflects the essential spirit of childhood and is an outgrowth of the artist's tireless study of the physiology, psychology, and behavior of infants and young boys and girls. "Actually, my dolls look very much like my own children when they were small," she

told us. "I like crafting boy dolls as much as girl dolls, but most collectors prefer girls."

In 1982, Sylvia Natterer exhibited her first limited-edition porcelain dolls - a 10½in (24cm) baby and two older girl dolls, one 15in (38cm), the other 16in (40cm) - at the Frankfurt Fair. The doll-crafting process the artist uses today is similar to that used for those first, prize-winning children.

Every Sylvia Natterer doll begins as a simple lump of clay and, for the artist, the rest is as exciting as opening a surprise package. "I can't wait to find out what's inside, and I don't stop modelling till the head is finished." When the head is completed, Sylvia constructs a two-part or four-part mold into which she pours porcelain limited editions of 30 or less for each prototype model. Features, including eyes, are painted with porcelain colors, after which the doll head is fired three

When grownups aren't looking, mayhem, in this case a pillow-fight free-for-all, breaks out in Doll Land! Twins are 13in (32cm) tall. *Photograph courtesy of Sylvia Natterer.*

Caught in the act! "How can someone as angelic as me do *anything* naughty?" (Every experienced Mom knows the answer to that one!) *Photograph courtesy of Sylvia Natterer.*

times. For black or Asiatic dolls, the artist applies skin tone with a sponge to achieve a soft, natural look. Some doll bodies are porcelain; most are cotton fabric stuffed with acrylic batting. Wigs are human hair, mohair or, occasionally, fur.

Costumes are crafted from the artist's original patterns, using contemporary fabrics and trims. Her dolls are modern children and wear modern clothes. For each costume design, Sylvia sews a prototype from which her sister-in-law, Griseldis, crafts garments for the dolls in the series. Stockings are handknitted; handcrafted leather shoes are often made by Sylvia herself.

Sylvia Natterer's dolls are quietly elegant, stylized and charming. "That's the effect I wish to achieve," she said emphatically. "In my work, I try to simplify, to avoid details like creases and wrinkles at the corners of eyes and mouths. I want my dolls to look like dolls, not humans in disguise!"

A variant of Sylvia's beloved theme, 21in (52cm) big sister takes charge of younger siblings. Sylvia had fun designing mohair wigs for these quadruplets! *Photograph courtesy of Sylvia Natterer.*

In this dream sequence the artist turns experience inside out. The *dreamer* appears unreal in her fairytale white lace, soft blue silk sash and elaborately-styled pale gold hair. The *dream*, by contrast, is a wistful 3-D Harlequin whose costume is strong and dominant. *Photograph courtesy of Sylvia Natterer.*

Tamara Neumann

A number of contemporary artists couple dollmaking with a second, very different career. For sheer contrast, however, few can match the two-track professional drama lived by 23-year-old Tamara Neumann. Tamara makes what are probably the smallest top-quality artist dolls presently being crafted in Germany. She is also a flight attendant with Lufthansa, is working toward a co-pilot's license, and is as much in love with travel/adventure as she is with the plastic arts.

This remarkable young lady is the daughter of a physicist and a painter, and it is from her artist mother that Tamara inherited her talent and received her early training. "As a child, I worked alongside my mother to craft beautiful figures for our Christmas crèche," Tamara told the authors. "My dollmaking grew out of such projects. I remember I had the idea to use my little sister as a model for a crèche shepherdess. When it was completed, it became my first doll."

Tamara developed her studio art with extraordinary speed. While still in her teens she exhibited her work regularly at doll shows. On several occasions, in fact, the artist's mother had to man the show table while Tamara attended class at her high school. After graduation from the lycée, Tamara enrolled in a market management training program, but her passion for travel led her to abandon marketing and join a motor expedition that crossed the Sahara from the Mediterranean to West Africa. The adventure proved so thrilling that she switched career tracks to make travel part of her job. Her present work for Lufthansa satisfies Tamara's "wanderlust" yet leaves large blocks of off-duty time open for doll crafting. "And each time I visit a new city with Lufthansa, I save one day for visits to local museums," she said enthusiastically. "It's a fantastic opportunity and impacts directly on my own art."

Tamara Neumann dolls, which average 8in (20cm) tall, represent young girls between the ages of 13-16. Occasionally, when a client insists, she will craft a boy/girl pair. The dolls are exquisitely detailed but rarely smile. "At their age, they already sense what the future holds for them," the artist confided. "The adult experience is no laughing matter."

Head, hands, and feet for every doll are molded in a porcelain-like material and derive from a set of five sculpted wax prototypes. Since the dolls are so very small — each head measures a scant $5/8$in-$3/4$in (2cm-2.5cm) — components must be sanded until they are silk smooth. Only then does Tamara apply a flesh tone acrylic base coat which she carefully overpaints with the rose blush cheeks, exquisitely-detailed eyes, and delicate lips that give life to her tiny people. "I create through my paintbrush, not through sculpted surfaces," the artist said. "The eyes must be able to speak. If I make one mistake, if my brush is too heavy with water and an iris smudges, I throw the head away. To minimize such disasters, I've developed a special breathing technique that allows my hands to remain absolutely steady while I paint."

Doll legs and hands are attached with steel wire wrapped around with elasticized fabric to give form and dimension to the body. Fine hair wigs are tinted, cut, and styled by the artist; design and color choice for a doll's costume are inspired by the color of its wig. Dainty period clothes are handsewn by Tamara who combs flea markets and fabric shops for suitable old and new yard goods. She will only use old lace trims, however, since "the antique laces are invariably finer than the modern ones." Completed dolls are nostalgic, long-ago little people, a curious counterpoint to the artist's own very contemporary lifestyle and jet-age career with Lufthansa. She has no ambition to produce a wide range of doll types. Rather, she tries to imbue each small masterpiece with a special flavor, a magic quality that unmistakably marks it as a genuine *Tamara-Puppe*.

We asked Tamara why she doesn't work in larger scales, use handblown glass eyes, ready-made wigs, or employ studio assistants to increase productivity and make her own life less arduous. "I want to do everything with my own hands," she explained. "Other dollmakers may use the services of glassblowers, wigmakers and dressmakers. Personally, I feel all that distances the artist from one-on-one creative experience. I want to craft each of my dolls completely by myself, to know that with a paintbrush, a handful of powdered porcelain, and a few scraps of cloth, I can create an artist doll in miniature who regards the observer calmly and reveals her sensitivity — like a female Tom Thumb from the old story."

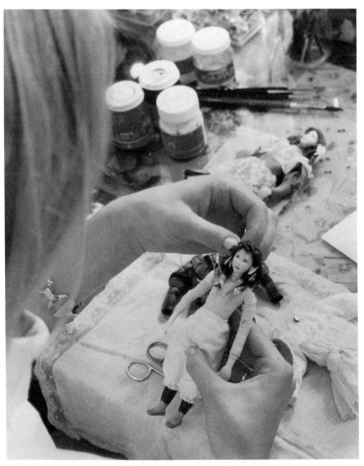

Tamara has begun to craft Judith's costume, a complex confection handsewn from her own patterns. Note the neat construction of the doll's body. Head, hands, and feet are attached by wire wrapped around with special elasticized fabric. *Photograph courtesy of Tamara Neumann.*

"The styling and coloration of each doll costume is totally dependent on the style and color of the wig," Tamara explained. Pictured is the completed Judith doll. *Photograph courtesy of Tamara Neumann.*

"I give expression to my dolls' faces through my paintbrush, not my carving tools," Tamara said. "To achieve perfect detail on a surface that measures 1in (3cm) or less is a thrilling challenge. To paint the eyes alone requires several hours of concentrated work. *Photograph courtesy of Tamara Neumann.*

8in (20cm) Maria is magnificently costumed in a black dress and fur-trimmed jacket handsewn by the artist. Tiny painted boots and a stunning muff complete her ensemble. *Photograph courtesy of Tamara Neumann.*

The costumes of Sonja and her little friend Esther are constructed from old and new fabrics, but all laces are antique. "Old lace is much finer than new," the artist said. Tamara makes everything herself, including the straw hats worn by her *puppen.* *Photograph courtesy of Tamara Neumann.*

Regina, an old fashioned teenager whose eyes and serious expression look toward the reality of adult life, but whose hands cling (literally) to childhood, epitomizes the moment of transition Tamara, herself only in her twenties, strives to capture through the plastic arts. *Photograph courtesy of Tamara Neumann.*

Detail of previous illustration.

Elisabeth Pongratz

Starting with the logo *Neue Münchner Künstlerpuppen* (New Munich Art Dolls), Elisabeth Pongratz extended the tradition established early in the century to craft durable, playable, artist-quality dolls for children to handle, love, and make the companions of their nursery years. In the spirit of predecessors like Käthe Kruse, Marion Kaulitz, Sasha Morgenthaler, Margarete Steiff, and commercial firms like Heubach and Kämmer & Reinhardt, who created playable dolls for youngsters growing up during the original Puppenreform movement, Elisabeth's work delights both adult and child collectors.

This artist, who holds degrees in sculpture and plastic arts from the Munich Academy of Fine Arts, has herself written extensively about the early Puppenreform movement. Like the old artists whose lives and works she finds fascinating, Elisabeth began crafting dolls for her own children and resolved early on to work only with all-natural materials. She

Elisabeth Pongratz's New Munich Art Dolls are intended, like their early-20th-century predecessors, to be lovable, playable children's toys. They are coveted by adult collectors as well, who admire their clean lines, fine design, and brilliant craftsmanship. *Photograph courtesy of Elisabeth Pongratz.*

experimented with clay and cloth before choosing wood as her preferred medium. With her husband, a medical doctor and anesthesiologist, she developed the construction methods and stylistic features, a unique blend of whimsy with superb art, that characterize her dolls.

Whether a doll is destined to be an all-wooden, spring-jointed child or a darling baby with carved, delicately-painted wooden head and stuffed fabric body, every Elisabeth Pongratz doll starts life in the clay barrel. The artist sculpts the prototype in clay, from which bronze castings are made of the doll's head, body, arms, and legs. These, in turn, are rough copied on a wood carving machine.

When machine-carved linden or maple components are removed from the carving machine, the artist refines the sculpture, adds detail carving and takes advantage of the highly-individual wood-grain patterns that characterize this classic and very dynamic medium. The finished sculpture is sanded to remove rough spots; then the face is overlaid with a pale, transparent wash through which the graining pattern of the underlying wood remains clearly visible. Features are painted, with particular care given to fine detail and depth of expression of the eyes. A few of Elisabeth's child dolls and all her babies have painted hair; most older children have real (animal fiber) hair or mohair wigs.

Final assembly of the all-wood spring-jointed dolls is completed on a special table designed by Wolf Pongratz, Elisabeth's husband. The doll is positioned on a wooden frame and clamped firmly in place. Steel springs are installed and access holes are plugged with wooden pegs. Baby dolls from this studio have wooden heads and fabric bodies filled with sand to simulate the weight distribution and feel of living infants. Instinctively, one reaches to support the tiny wooden head that rocks realistically backward on its sturdy cotton body.

The artist's preference for natural materials includes costume fabric and genuine leather for doll shoes. In an article published in *Doll Reader*® magazine in November, 1985, author Rhonda Everett Weinstein wrote that Elisabeth Pongratz dolls wear white cotton-knit undergarments and either classic cotton outfits or coats, sweaters, and bonnets handknitted from pure wool by the artist's talented mother. Like her dolls, designs for the artist's doll costumes are astringent and free of frills. There are few accessories, no lace, ribbon, or rickrack trim. Closures for tiny sweaters, dresses, and overalls are in-scale, finely-sanded hardwood buttons.

Elisabeth's dolls are particularly coveted by Japanese collectors whose culture and tradition share much with the artist's aesthetic philosophy. Americans sense a kinship with Shaker art in the dolls' clean, exposed lines. For children and adults worldwide, however, Elisabeth Pongratz dolls speak to the heart, with their haunting expression and endearing design. Like all first-rate art, their appeal is, in the end, universal.

Since this artist works hard to extend the early-20th-century concept of the doll as a cuddle-able friend of childhood, she is particularly pleased about her partnership, since1991/

Don't be fooled by the apparent simplicity of design of these dolls from Elisabeth's studio. Each is a subtle example of the dollmaker's art that leaves no room for error. Japanese collectors find them particularly appealing since the artist's aesthetic is similar to that of Eastern art. *Photograph courtesy of Elisabeth Pongratz.*

1992, with American dealer/manufacturer and personal friend, Rhonda Weinstein, who has helped make Pongratz dolls more affordable for today's children.

Rhonda Weinstein is licensed by Dr. and Mrs. Pongratz to manufacturer boy and girl dolls that average 10in (25cm) tall, using designs and a prototype head supplied by the artist in Germany. At the "New Munich Art Dolls Co.," doll heads were first carved in basswood, which has recently been replaced by maple. Doll faces are painted; boy dolls receive mohair wigs while girls have natural animal fiber hair. Bodies are dense cotton fabric stuffed with shredded cotton fabric. Each doll is fitted with cardboard hip joints similar to those found inside traditional teddy bears. Costumes are natural fabrics, in accord with Elisabeth Pongratz's preference for natural materials. These "Pongratz" dolls crafted as a cottage industry in Virginia, U.S.A., were, as of February 1993, only sold through select shops in Europe, but Elisabeth and her American friend hope the dolls will soon become available for purchase in the United States as well.

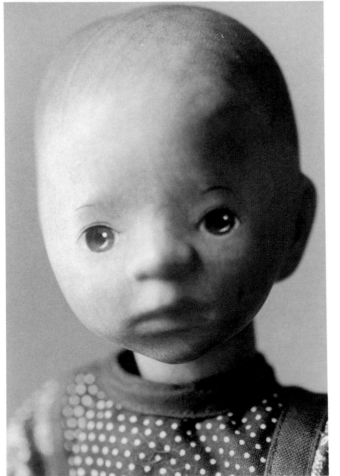

Top: This charming boy, with his bushy human hair wig, wears a soft brown sweater handknit by the artist's talented mother. Doll faces receive an initial wash of transparent flesh tone that leaves the underlying wood grain visible. The base coat is overlaid with detail painting, with particular attention paid to dolls' eyes. *Photograph courtesy of Elisabeth Pongratz.*

Bottom: All of Elisabeth's babies have painted hair. Here, the artist has painted the hair of an older child, a detail that adds astringency to the overall design. All-wood children from this studio range from 10in (24cm) to 14in (36cm) tall. *Photograph courtesy of Elisabeth Pongratz.*

Adorable twins pause to hug in a summer meadow. Whether Elisabeth's dolls wear knitted garments or artist-designed cloth costumes, their outfits have the same purity of design and lack of frills that characterize the dolls. *Photograph courtesy of Elisabeth Pongratz.*

A creamy-white mohair wig and delicate floral wreath lend touches of magic to this darling child. Despite appearances, the dolls are sturdy and durable. They easily survive the rough and tumble of their young owners' childhood years, the artist told us. *Photograph courtesy of Elisabeth Pongratz.*

Dolls manufactured by the New Munich Art Dolls Co. based in Virginia, USA, are licensed by Elisabeth Pongratz, who supplies the company with designs for heads, bodies, and clothing patterns. Elisabeth is delighted that this partnership, with American dealer/manufacturer Rhonda Weinstein, makes dolls in the early-20th-century tradition more accessible to today's children. *Photograph courtesy of the New Munich Art Dolls Co.*

Three all-wood youngsters with painted hair and soft beige outfits handknitted by the artist's mother. Note the "mitten hands" typical of Elisabeth Pongratz's work. *Photograph courtesy of Elisabeth Pongratz.*

Carla Rauser

"Since I love working with my hands, I made a doll for my sister's birthday ten years ago. I could have made any number of things for her, and it was sheer happenstance that I crafted a doll. But that project gave me such pleasure," artist Carla Rauser told the authors, "that from that day forward I couldn't stop making dolls. At first the craft aspect provided the challenge; then the concept of creating 'little people' became fascinating, and I worked harder and harder to create dolls with the personalities and expressive features of living children."

Carla Rauser had little interest in dolls during her childhood years. She owned several *Barbies®* but didn't enjoy playing with them. "I liked to design and sew their clothes," she told us, "but the real love of my childhood was playing with my big toy kitchen and mastering the art of cooking." As a young adult, Carla trained as a paralegal, then worked as a secretary for a transport firm for 13 years. But after creating her sister's birthday doll in 1985, the new hobby consumed more and more of the artist's time and energy until, one day in 1990, Carla walked away from her office desk to become a full-time dollmaker. "I have never regretted that decision," she declared.

Carla Rauser's early dolls were crafted from Cernit® or natural clay, but since 1987 she has worked exclusively with porcelain. She makes some portrait dolls, but most of her work is inspired by photographs of children or evolves from composite images shaped in her own imagination. Each doll begins as a lump of clay which the artist forms with her hands and fingers, using sculpting tools only for the more subtle detail carving. When a new head is completed, Carla makes a two-part mold from the prototype, then pours the porcelain for one or more dolls. "I don't sculpt a new head for each doll unless I'm doing a portrait piece," she said. "Instead, I prefer to start with a basic head, then change and refine it to create an individual. It's very important to me that each of my dolls have a unique personality, be a person in its own right."

Carla keeps assorted styles and sizes of molds for doll arms and legs in the studio and periodically replaces these with new molds as her dollmaking skill improves. Doll bodies are cotton fabric stuffed with acrylic batting. Occasionally, dolls are constructed around wire armatures and are fully posable. Features are painted with porcelain colors mixed with a water-based medium, to produce the soft tones favored by the artist. Eyes are crystal (*Kristallaugen*). Wigs are natural human hair for child dolls and fine mohair for infants and toddlers.

Carla Rauser dolls, for the 90s, belong to our contemporary scene. The artist takes pains to ensure that colors, patterns, and styling of garments worn by her children coordinate with their hair, eyes, and personalities. As time permits,

A darling baby from Carla Rauser's studio. The 14in (35cm) youngster has a porcelain head, arms, and legs and a cotton fabric body stuffed with acrylic batting. *Photograph courtesy of Carla Rauser.*

Above left: "At first the craft aspect provided the challenge; then the concept of creating little people became fascinating, and I worked harder and harder to craft dolls with the personalities and expressive features of living children." *Photograph courtesy of Carla Rauser.*

Above right: Dolls from this studio are painted with porcelain colors mixed with a special water-based medium to give the soft tonal quality favored by the artist. Child dolls have wigs made from human hair; infant and toddler wigs are mohair. *Photograph courtesy of Carla Rauser.*

Left: This relaxed, realistic 30in (75cm) boy doll looks like the product of a logical, orderly studio. But when Carla is at work, emotions take over completely and, by day's end, the studio looks as though a hurricane has passed through. "I think I need this chaos, that for me it's a vital part of the creative experience," Carla explained. *Photograph courtesy of Carla Rauser.*

Carla's children belong to our contemporary world and wear 1990s fashions. As time permits, the artist designs and sews all her doll clothes herself. When help is needed, Carla calls upon her mother, a gifted needleartist with taste similar to her own. *Photograph courtesy of Carla Rauser.*

Japanese boy/girl twins 24in (60cm) tall. Like many of today's top European artists, Carla Rauser enjoys the challenge of faces and cultures different from her own. *Photograph courtesy of Carla Rauser.*

she sews their costumes herself. When help is needed, Carla's mother joins her in the studio. The women work well together and have similar artistic taste.

The 14-30in (35-75cm) dolls from this Ratingen studio have an air of refinement and elegance that suggests remarkable logic, control, and orderliness in the workshop. In fact, nothing could be farther from the truth. "That is my studio philosophy, but unfortunately it's a philosophy in theory only," Carla told us with an amused smile. "The truth is that when I work, my emotions take over completely; an inner force is unleashed. In the evening, after a day in the studio, the room resembles the aftermath of a hurricane, and the next day I spend at least an hour putting things away and making the place livable again. Sometimes, though, I think I need this chaos, that for me it's a vital part of the creative experience," the artist added thoughtfully. "I believe disorder stimulates me."

A 1992 Carla Rauser baby doll in porcelain, photographed on the sunny balcony of its present home in Paris, France. The doll is 20in (50cm) tall. *Photograph courtesy of Ingeborg Riesser.*

An unusual piece, this porcelain bust crafted in 1992 is 7in (18cm) high. *Photograph courtesy of Ingeborg Riesser.*

Regina & Abhinavo Sandreuter

The distinctive faces of wood and porcelain dolls from the Munich studio of Regina and Abhinavo Sandreuter are a modern extension of an old dollmaking tradition. "We like the idea that a doll's face should appear unspecific and calm, to mirror the changing moods of the onlooker," Regina told us. "We try to give our dolls a look that is *on the verge* of expression rather than a particular expression. In the same way, our dolls' costumes don't reflect a 'fixed' period or style in fashion history. And their 8- or 12-part MultiPose® bodies permit the collector to position each doll in innumerable lifelike attitudes; the figures aren't frozen sculptures."

The purity of expression and fluid body design that characterize Sandreuter dolls are end products of a decade of experimentation and a single-minded effort to perfect that art form. Regina and Abhinavo come to dollmaking from very different backgrounds. Regina trained as a translator, then switched to film set decoration. Abhinavo studied the graphic arts and says that "after having designed two-dimensional printed items for years, the jump into the third dimension was and still is a challenge." The couple met in India in 1981 and, following their return to Europe, began to look for work that would draw on their combined background and experience. A friend suggested dollmaking and they decided to give it a try.

The Sandreuters quickly graduated from Cernit® to synthetic resin as the material from which to model doll heads. Early dolls had stuffed cloth bodies and wore rainbow-hued soft cotton fabrics and turbans adorned with feathers. From the beginning, the couple liked the unisex look of baggy trousers and a slightly-theatrical eastern atmosphere. "Our 'passage to India' probably played a role in our attitude toward costume design," Regina confessed.

The difficulties encountered during early efforts to market their dolls are detailed in the article Regina wrote for the 1990 NIADA Convention. There, she describes long evenings in Schwabing, Munich's famous artist street, where the dolls received lavish praise from onlookers but there were few sales. Those summer evenings brought two pieces of valuable advice, however. One was to apply for membership at the Bavarian Arts and Crafts Institute; the other was to apply at the Ludwig Beck Department Store in Munich for a place in the store's well-known December craft show.

The Sandreuters were accepted by the Crafts Institute and by Ludwig Beck where, as an annual holiday sales promotional, sections of each floor were transformed into "living workshops." "The second floor was reserved for the dollmakers," Regina recounted in *Convention Highlights: The Sandreuter Saga* (NIADA 1990). "Until that first December at Ludwig

A 17½in (44cm) wooden doll with 8-part MultiPose® body, mohair wig, cotton-and-wool clothes with silk-embroidered detail, and elegant leather boots. *Photograph by Jörg Beske, Munich. Courtesy of Regina & Abhinavo Sandreuter.*

Beck," the artist continued, "we had no contact with other dollmakers. Now we discovered that there existed a whole subculture of dollmakers and doll collectors. Names didn't mean anything to me then, but a glance at the program for 1982, with artists like Brigitte Deval, Hildegard Günzel, Annette Himstedt, to list just a few, shows what a breeding ground for dollmakers Beck's Christmas Show was at that time."

Event followed event and the Sandreuters' reputation for excellence grew among discriminating collectors. Munich doll artist Sylvia Natterer introduced their work to our co-author, Ingeborg Riesser, who was about to open her shop in Paris. Regina and Abhinavo were invited to display their dolls in the crafts section of the Frankfurt International Fair. But along with the welcome influx of orders came a new and serious problem. "By then, our dolls had wooden bodies," Regina said, "but their heads, hands, and feet were made of synthetic resin, a two-component compound that released toxic fumes when we poured our molds. For our own safety, we had always performed this task outdoors, but the pressure of increased numbers of orders and sales deadlines made it impractical to work only in good weather. We realized we had to switch to a medium that posed no health threat, and that's when we began working with wood, the material we've used ever since, along with our recent work in porcelain."

Surely, the Sandreuter's studio process is unique in the world! Each doll begins as a life-size or larger head modelled in clay. The clay piece is cast in plaster, which is easier to refine and finish, and the completed plaster head is sent to a bronze caster. The bronze model is further refined, then serves as a master model for the woodcarving machine, which cuts maple replicas of 3-D forms in the desired reduced scale, much as a pantograph draws in-scale replicas of line drawings on paper. "The carving machine reproduces the forms of our models quite well," Regina said. "Fine details of eyes, nostrils, and lips are lost in the process, however, and must be carved by hand directly into the maple wood. In the end, the character of a doll is greatly affected by this work with knife and scalpel and the finishing with sandpaper. The handwork makes each doll unique, even though we work from a limited number of bronze masters."

Wood doll components are primed, then painted with Winsor & Newton Artist's Alkyd Colors®; porcelain dolls are painted with porcelain colors. Doll eyes are

Top: Note the exotic elements of the boy and girl dolls' contemporary-styled costumes. "A preference for trousers may date from our experience in India," Regina told us. *Photograph by Jörg Beske, Munich. Courtesy of Regina & Abhinavo Sandreuter.*

Bottom: A stunning child doll whose costume complements the deep red of her elaborate mohair wig. Eight and 12-joint bodies enable the dolls to assume acitve lifelike poses. Here, the young lady actually seems to roll her hoop. *Photograph by Jörg Beske, Munich. Courtesy of Regina & Abhinavo Sandreuter.*

The Sandreuters introduced their 12-part, all-porcelain MultiPose® dolls at the Nuremberg Toy Fair in 1993. Each doll has all the beauty of design that characterizes the artists' woodens, and is enhanced by the silk-smooth quality of porcelain. *Photograph by Jörg Beske, Munich. Courtesy of Regina & Abhinavo Sandreuter.*

painted, not glass, and completed faces receive a coat of protective varnish. Wigs are custom-crafted from mohair; parts are handknotted. The artists prefer mohair to human-hair wigs as the individual fibers are finer and better scaled for diminutive doll heads. "Collectors may be interested to learn that mohair wigs cost us much more than similar wigs made of human-hair," Regina said. "It's a mistake to think that human-hair wigs are invariably more expensive."

Doll costumes are natural fabrics, often intricately patterned. The artists are especially fond of traditional and modern Ikat fabrics and described the "agony and ecstasy" of searching for buttons and leathers that coordinate with the striking, offbeat dyes characteristic of this cloth. Doll outfits are contemporary art designs that are neither fashionably modern nor nostalgically old fashioned. Garments have a slightly exotic flavor and are a satisfying blend of color, texture and design. Much of the sewing of doll clothes and shoes is done by studio helpers.

Among the distinctive features that characterize wood and porcelain dolls from the Sandreuters' Munich studio are elaborate MultiPose® jointed bodies that enable dolls to assume numerous lifelike positions. The artists' original wooden body, still in production, has eight components and, like more recent designs, is assembled with elastic cords. Regina and Abhinavo have even designed a 12-part body which enables dolls to bend arms and grasp objects. Sculpted clay masters for doll heads, reworked in plaster, bronze, wood, and sometimes in porcelain, are used for boy as well as girl dolls since, in the artists' opinion, "apart from hair style and clothes, it is hard to tell whether the face of a child under a certain age belongs to a boy or girl."

Regina admits that, over the years, art she has purchased for her own small and select collection has always featured the human form. Since she and Abhinavo became doll artists, their fine arts interest has become increasingly focused on sculpture. Their own dolls, although not portraits of individual children, are kinetic sculptures that combine empathy with the spirit of childhood and an instinct for outstanding design characteristic of first-rate art.

At center stage on a slate-blue bench is a 16½in (43cm) 12-part porcelain doll dressed and accessorized in a blend of "mod" and bold fantasy. *Photograph by Jörg Beske, Munich. Courtesy of Regina & Abhinavo Sandreuter.*

A trio of Sandreuter dolls perform lifelike actions — walking and riding a scooter. The artists' work provides exquisite contrast. On the one hand, their dolls simulate realistic human motion to an extraordinary degree. On the other, doll faces are intentionally remote, contained, removed from the fluid expressions that characterize living children. *Photograph by Jörg Beske, Munich. Courtesy of Regina & Abhinavo Sandreuter.*

A delightful 12-part MultiPose® wooden doll crafted in 1993. As always, the exquisite integration of coloring, hair, fabric and accessories give this Sandreuter doll a life of its own. *Photograph by Jörg Beske, Munich. Courtesy of Regina & Abhinavo Sandreuter.*

Karin Schmidt

Like many of today's artists, Karin Schmidt mourns the lost dolls of her own childhood. "When I was small, I had a cloth doll named Peter whom I loved dearly but who was lost during the war. Later, my mother gave me a celluloid doll that accompanied me everywhere. It was my confidential friend! But when I reached 14," the artist told us sadly, "my mother gave my doll away without consulting me. The shock of loss gave birth to a love, a passion for dolls, a feeling that began in my teens but which I only began to understand years later."

Karin has no formal training in the arts and, as a dollmaker, she is completely self-taught. She studied commerce and trained for the very practical profession of office manager. But after marriage and the birth of her first child, she experienced a resurgence of love for dolls, particularly the gorgeous 19th-century porcelain bébés that bring top dollars at auction. "I dreamed of possessing one, perhaps two of these exquisite creatures, but they were beyond my means. 'Do it yourself,' a voice seemed to whisper, and that was when I discovered creativity and the creative power I never knew I had."

It was the beginning of an adventure in self-discovery. There were tears and laughter in equal measure during the years when she taught herself the dollmaker's art. "I adopted the motto 'Learn from your own mistakes', and there were certainly plenty of them!" But as she gained in experience and control of her medium, Karin's excitement grew. She was startled to see the quality art she could produce, that her hands actually had power to give three-dimensional form to her dreams. "That was when I decided to define my limits, to create at the outermost edge of my talent," she explained. "I wanted to explore, to find what lay within me. And I wanted to create very special portrait dolls of children, working from photographs and from composite images that evolved within my own imagination."

Today, Karin crafts her porcelain artist dolls in a cheery studio bathed in sunlight. Dolls measuring 26-31in (65-80cm) have porcelain arms, legs, heads and shoulderplates. Her 18in (45cm) babies have legs crafted entirely from porcelain and porcelain arms to the elbows. Doll bodies are linen stuffed with sheep wool. Most of the dolls are one-of-a-kinds, but

Karin's based her delightful Goose Girl on an old German folk tale. A human hair wig styled by the artist frames the child's face. Karin's one-of-a-kind *gänseliesel* (goose girl) is 32in (80cm) tall and wears an outfit designed and sewn by Karin herself. *Photograph courtesy of Karin Schmidt.*

Detail of previous illustration. Karin's Goose Girl is at the same time innocent and worldly-wise. Observe the determined lines of her exquisitely-feathered eyebrows, the firm set of the lips. *Photograph courtesy of Karin Schmidt.*

late in 1991 Karin designed three limited editions of 30 as a first experiment in series dollmaking.

Karin's dolls are painted with waterbase porcelain colors. Eyes are handblown glass; wigs are human hair or mohair. "Over the years, I've amassed a huge collection of precious fabrics, ribbons, laces and accessories," she said. "This gives me great creative freedom when designing doll costumes. I personally sew every garment worn by my one-of-a-kinds; clothes worn by the series dolls are made to my specifications by a professional dressmaker. And a piece of luck came my way," she added, "when a gifted older lady saw my work and fell in love with it. She frequently enhances doll costumes with details that lend them an air of enchantment."

Karin Schmidt's personality has a roguish side that is reflected in her dolls. "I'm glad they have the same moods I do — obstinacy, anger, melancholy, joy, audacity." And although Karin crafts children like her *gänseliesel* (goose girl) and the friends, Sophie and Toni, whose ethnic origin is clearly the artist's native Germany, she is increasingly drawn to boys and girls from Third World nations. She is fascinated by farmers and villagers whose lifestyle perpetuates tradition in the face of an encroaching hi-tech world. "I'm attracted by the native peoples of South America, Africa, and Asia," she told us. "To create a doll that is an honest statement about such cultures is tremendously enriching. Such projects require intensive research about the country, the people, their culture and their history."

Each doll from this German studio has something very important to say. It makes direct eye contact with the observer; its lips seem ready to speak. The illusion is critical to her work, Karin insists. It is how she fulfills her moral responsibility to the art object. "A doll is powerless to communicate ideas through spoken words," she explained, "so the artist must pay special attention to the sculpting of the mouth, the contours of the eyelids. Dolls express their souls through their eyes and lips."

In this she succeeds to an uncanny degree. Baby Mario is an intense and beautiful child who gazes solemnly at the viewer from his Latin American village world. His lips and eyes speak to us with the power of the voice he lacks. They tell a tale of love and care in eternal conflict with hardship and

28in (70cm) Sancha was "born" the day Karin met a little Chilean girl in the tumult of a German Christmas Fair. The artist sculpted facial detail directly into the porcelain for this one-of-a-kind masterpiece. Artist-designed wig and costume reinforce the individuality of this determined little lady. *Photograph courtesy of Karin Schmidt.*

"My dolls want to communicate with the observer; they have something to say," Karin told us, and little Mario, the artist's adorable wee lad from Chile, is a case in point. His personality and message belie his diminutive 18in (45cm) size, an effect heightened by the dramatic treatment of the wig. *Photograph courtesy of Karin Schmidt.*

deprivation, an endless struggle for subsistence survival that blurs the childhood dreams of Third World babies.

Among Karin's most dramatic one-of-a-kind Third World dolls is Sancha, who evolved from a chance meeting with a Chilean girl in the tumult of a recent German Christmas Fair. "That encounter inspired Sancha," the artist said, "a solemn girl doll filled to bursting with life force and a generous dose of self-confidence. I sculpted the facial details directly into the porcelain. The wig and garments are my own creation and part of the artistic statement."

As with all Karin Schmidt dolls, Mario and Sancha wear costumes that complement their personalities and enhance their message. Mario's unkempt hair and colorful poncho enclose him in a cultural cocoon from which he stares out at us with strength mingled with sorrow. Sancha's vitality depends in large measure on the subtlety of her costume; the droop of the leather cape echoes the drooping lines of her young mouth. Each doll's expression is reinforced through details of clothing, and with Sancha, accessories are just as meaningful. Her necklace of exotic berries and dried corn, the wooden beads looped through her coarse black hair — such details are calculated to heighten the sense of the exotic, to complete the bond between ethnic culture and living child.

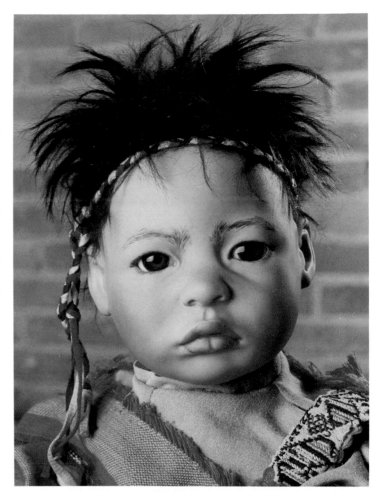

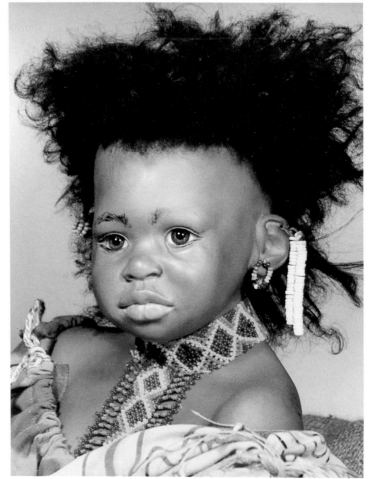

Top: Detail of previous illustration. Mario's lips and eyes speak to us as powerfully as the voice he lacks. They tell a tale of love and care mixed with hardship, and a struggle for survival that blurs the childhood dreams of Third World babies. *Photograph courtesy of Karin Schmidt.*

Bottom: "The eyes and lips are the soul of a doll," asserts artist Karin Schmidt. The soul of this one-of-a-kind young African girl is spelled out in every detail of her face, wig, costume, and accessories. The child, crafted in 1992 and named Rasheeda by the artist, measures 26in (65cm) tall. *Photograph courtesy of Karin Schmidt.*

Tamala, a 26in (65cm) one-of-a-kind porcelain child crafted in 1992, is another Third World personality from Karin's studio. The complex design of the wig, the ragged stole, and the woven necklace, all point to a chaotic, impoverished Latin existence in which this little girl desperately struggles to establish an orderly pattern. *Photograph courtesy of Karin Schmidt.*

Karin creates one-of-a-kind and limited-edition children from her native Germany in addition to her Third World youngsters. Here are Sophie and Toni, two cheerful Bavarians, each 30in (75cm) tall. Toni has caught sight of the photographer, but Sophie remains absorbed in her own thoughts. *Photograph courtesy of Karin Schmidt.*

Vera Scholz

As a child, Vera Scholz enjoyed playing with dolls, especially dolls with beautiful long hair, since her secret dream was to possess such hair herself. When she was nine, she acquired her first antique doll, a beauty retrieved from the top of a neighbor's trash bin. The doll was about 24in (61cm) tall and in excellent condition, with a jointed body and a lovely porcelain head, brown glass eyes, and long blond hair. "I adored the doll's face but disliked her body," the artist told us. "Eventually, to my sorrow, that wonderful doll disappeared. I think my mother must have thrown her back into the trash barrel!" As a teenager, Vera Scholz saw many similar dolls at local flea markets but, despite their modest prices, she lacked funds to purchase them.

In 1972, Vera Scholz decided to craft the dolls she couldn't afford to buy. First efforts had large eyes, fat cheeks, and tiny, heart-shaped mouths, features that echoed the beloved toy recalled from childhood. She found old glass eyes at the flea market and crafted wigs from flax or discarded hairpieces fashionable during the 70s. "Those early dolls were quite horrible," the artist confided to the authors, "but at the time I thought they were lovely. I sold some and threw others away later on."

From girlhood, Vera has loved to work with her hands and dreamed of a career in fashion design. But she fell out of love with the field during a three-year apprenticeship at a Hamburg studio and turned her attention instead to the studio arts — oil painting, pastels and water colors. After two years of rigorous training, she exhibited her work in Hamburg and, later, in Buxtehude. Her art was well received and she opened a small private painting studio, but something, she told us, kept pulling her back toward the doll world she had never ceased to find fascinating. Her students urged her to add doll sculpting to the course offerings at the studio. She did, but soon became so involved with doll sculpture and experiments with every conceivable medium that she shut down the school and gave in to the inevitable.

Once the artist accepted the fact that she was a born dollmaker, she put memories of antique dolls behind her and gave free rein to her own creative imagination. She crafted child dolls and adult dolls, "punk" dolls and dream dolls with feathers for hair and paper clothing. She made small traditional dolls and fantastic marionettes over 1m (39in) high, in a relentless search for the style and focus that are her own. Vera, who first experimented with porcelain in the 1980s, mastered this temperamental medium after much difficulty. Now she works with it exclusively.

Vera Scholz dolls are inspired by chance meetings with attractive, interesting children, by photos of children in magazines and, sometimes, by very private flights of fancy. Doll heads and legs are sculpted from clay or Plastillin®. Shoulders, arms, and hands are modelled in FIMO®. Vera's dolls are large, and it takes considerable strength and skill to handle

A small dreamer from Vera's studio cuddles a special friend. The artist uses human hair for most of her doll wigs. Her smallest dolls, however, have wigs made of mohair. "The finer fiber is better scaled to the size of the dolls." *Photograph courtesy of Vera Scholz.*

A 37in (94cm) darling from Vera's Buxtehude studio. Note the exquisite painted detail of skin, lips, and shadows. The artist uses French porcelain colors exclusively. *Photograph courtesy of Vera Scholz.*

the two to four part molds taken from sculpted prototypes. "I never use the same mold more than 20 times," the artist said firmly. "And as each porcelain head emerges from a given mold, I change it slightly, to individualize the doll while the material is soft. I make more changes after the porcelain has thoroughly dried, and I vary painted detail, eye color, wig style, and costumes within a single edition. My aim is to craft 20 *individuals* from a single prototype."

In recent years, Vera has only used French porcelain colors. Doll heads are fired twice; arms and legs are often fired twice as well, since she paints fingernails and toenails in realistic detail. Understandably, this artist loves beautifully crafted German glass eyes, but she will not compromise quality in her studio. When suitable glass eyes aren't available for a particular project ("sometimes the iris is too large; you can't see the white of the eye"), Vera crafts eyes herself from white Cernit®, fires them in her kiln, positions them in the doll's head and paints the iris with watercolors. Finished eyes receive two coats of high-gloss lacquer, glued-on upper lashes made of fiber, and painted lower lashes.

Patterns for doll costumes are designed and sewn by the artist. "I like romantic garments that are also simple, with a minimum of lace and fuss," she said. "I prefer new cotton fabrics with small, in-scale patterns, but I occasionally turn to silks and velvets if they are right for a particular project. The important thing, to me, is that the doll and its outfit form a unified, harmonious composition. Most of my dolls are large, from 30in (76cm) to 36in (90cm) and have human hair wigs which I style myself. For my smaller dolls, I prefer wigs made of mohair, since the finer fiber is better suited to the delicate scale of the work."

Regardless of size, Vera Scholz doll bodies are skin-tone cotton fabric stuffed with special cotton batting. The artist threads flat steel wires through each body and into hollow doll limbs to insure proper positioning of porcelain arms and legs. She loves her work and tries to avoid anything that smacks of commercialism. "I accept few commissions and try to work at my own natural rhythm," she told us. "I want my work to have a harmonious, peaceful, almost neutral aura, to create faces where changing emotions in the *viewer* are echoed in the features and expression of the doll. I dislike dolls with contorted faces, faces that appear to be shouting or crying.

When Vera first embarked on her career as a dollmaker, she envied artists who could afford to purchase magnificent wigs and glass eyes for their creations. "I never had much money and was grateful to sell one or two dolls so that I could restock my studio with basic materials," she said. "I reinvested the money I earned in fine wigs and accessories for the dolls rather than buying elegant clothes for myself.

Top: Skipper, like every Vera Scholz doll, wears a costume designed and sewn by the artist. "The doll and its outfit must form a unified, harmonious composition," she explained. *Photograph courtesy of Vera Scholz.*

Bottom: This adorable freckled redhead wears a neutral, enigmatic expression typical of Vera's dolls. Despite the remoteness, she is an active mischievous and bouncy youngster! *Photograph courtesy of Vera Scholz.*

The 32in (80cm) limited-edition Ka wears a beautiful checked dress with elaborate smocking. *Photograph courtesy of Vera Scholz.*

A wistful and very handsome Latin American boy. The 32in (80cm) doll is
one of an edition limited to 10.

Near life-size Korean boy. The harmony and peace Vera strives for in her work are particularly suited to Eastern subjects. *Photograph courtesy of Vera Scholz.*

Above left: A delicate, lovable Latin child, whose exquisitely-painted porcelain features are framed by a thick, dark human hair wig and highlighted by the colorful dress fabric. The girl stands 32in (80cm) tall. *Photograph courtesy of Vera Scholz.*

Above right: A bright and determined young lady! Observe how the child's face is framed by luxuriant straight dark hair and thick bangs. *Photograph courtesy of Vera Scholz.*

Right: A limited edition of 10 pieces worldwide, Su is adorable in her elegantly-smocked party dress and white bead necklace. Note the natural way in which the child's wavy hair rebels against Mama's tight braids! *Photograph courtesy of Vera Scholz.*

Rotraut Schrott

Incredible as it may appear to collectors in the 1990s, dollmaker *extraordinaire* Rotraut Schrott never intended a career in the arts. Rather, she studied languages, worked briefly in her chosen field, then married and settled into the comfortable housewife's world of homemaking and child rearing. Rotraut designed and sewed clothing — dresses, jackets and coats for herself, delightful outfits for her children. The exceptional quality of her work attracted the attention of neighbors and soon Rotraut was busy designing garments for *their* children as well as her own. For relaxation and as a change of pace during those demanding years, the future dollmaker enrolled in a sculpting class. "I had no way to foresee it of course," she said, "but that studio course was the ticket to my future!"

The "future" made itself known at Christmas 1980. Rotraut sculpted a small doll as a gift for a child and discovered her remarkable ability to "give life to the clay." Fascinated by the surprising power of her own hands, she began to sculpt seriously and set about mastering the complex world of dollmaking which from the first she knew would incorporate her love of antique and contemporary fabrics and fashion design.

Guidance and invaluable instruction in human anatomy came from her father, Ludwig Adam, a well-known German artist with over 45 years of experience as a professional portrait painter. It is this knowledge, translated from the two-dimensional world of the painter into the three-dimensional world of the sculptor, that gives life to Rotraut's dolls. They represent far more than the outward form of her subjects. Muscles appear to ripple beneath smooth young skin. Cheekbones give form to faces, and the viewer has the impression that instead of the classic dollmaker's armature of twisted

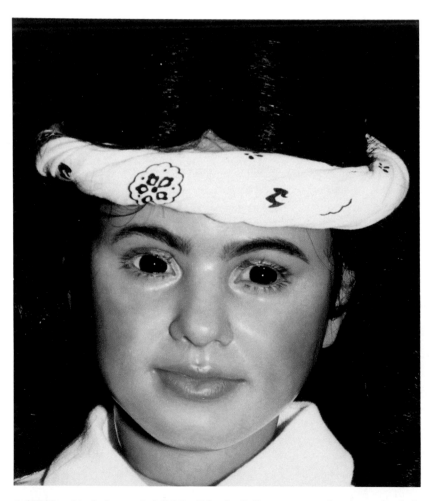

A 1991 handcrafted portrait doll 34in (86cm) tall. Do you recognize the young lady depicted here? She's tennis champion, Gabriela Sabatini, age 15. *Photograph courtesy of Rotraut Schrott.*

The actual photograph of Gabriela Sabatini from which the artist developed her portrait doll. "I think of my sculptures as 'children' and make them as realistic as possible," Rotraut told us. "That's why I especially enjoy doing portrait dolls."

Silja, 28in (70cm), was modelled directly in Cernit® in 1991. Eyes are painted. Silja's wig is custom crafted from European human hair. *Photograph courtesy of Rotraut Schrott.*

"When I develop a new piece, like Alice pictured here, I'm oblivious to the world beyond the studio," Rotraut said. "I focus on the doll's expression. Should this 'child' be playing with friends? Is she about to do something naughty? Is she lost in a world of dreams? Answers to these questions give life to the doll." *Photograph courtesy of Rotraut Schrott.*

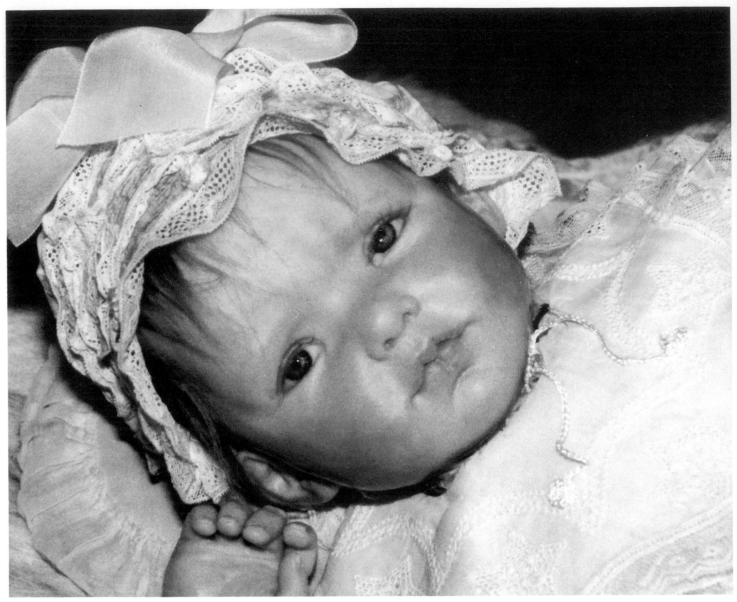

A 25in (64cm) baby doll made in 1987. The artist studied anatomy with her father, well-known German painter Ludwig Adam. The power of Rotraut's dolls to convey the mystique of living beings depends in large measure on her understanding of bone structure, musculature, the mechanics of the human body. *Photograph courtesy of Rotraut Schrott.*

steel wire, these dolls are living forms supported by inner skeletons of bone and cartilage. To master the details of human anatomy to such a degree required years of study and Rotraut admits there were moments when her patience frayed. "I want to be perfect straight away right from the beginning, and his criticisms [her father's] sometimes hurts me a bit,..." Rotraut Schrott told Ursula Driskell in a 1991 interview for *Doll Reader®*. "I still remember the battle we had about ears!"

In-depth knowledge of human anatomy provides the mechanics for Rotraut Schrott dolls; their depth of soul is directly inspired by the artist's life-long passion for old masters paintings. She loves Rembrandt, Titian, Botticelli, and Velasquez — her favorite, with his beautiful portraits of young royals in Renaissance Spain. "I admire the exquisite beauty of his drawing and the warmth of his faces, qualities I feel are lacking in even the finest antique dolls," she told the authors. "I try to use my skill as a sculptor to craft dolls that reflect what I love best in Velasquez' paintings."

For years, the artist has designed both limited edition porcelain and unlimited vinyl edition dolls for commercial manufacture and sale by GADCO®. Despite this involvement, which gives the middle-range collector access to her stunning work, Rotraut finds the greatest *personal* satisfaction crafting one-of-a-kind Cernit® children — some commissioned portraits of real-life youngsters, some dream children fantastically costumed, pure products of the artist's fertile imagination.

In her studio, Rotraut only makes one-of-a-kind dolls since she feels the entire limited-edition process — from clay prototype to moldmaking to numbered series of identically-finished dolls — inhibits creative experience. Rotraut prefers to craft individual works of art, just as a fine painter creates canvases one at a time. For this work, she sculpts directly in Cernit®. Each tiny crease in the lips, fine detail of eyelids and ears, and the subtle lines of the nose are meticulously carved with fine sticks or needles. Arms, legs, shoulders — all are crafted with precise attention to anatomical truth. "When I sculpt a new work, I forget the world around me," Rotraut told us. "The work of art becomes everything, and the face I am creating draws reality from my ideas of the moment. This child, should it be playing with friends? Is it about to do something naughty? Is the girl daydreaming? Or is she happily licking a lollipop, like my Silja? Is his mouth dirty? Is her nose freckled? Is this little boy winking at me? These are the thoughts that fill my mind."

The logic that makes Rotraut opt for one-of-a-kind studio dolls, where the artist retains complete control of the work being crafted, lies behind her preference for painted rather than handblown glass eyes. "Through painted eyes, I can convey greater warmth, vivacity, and realism," she explained. "My dolls' eyes are painted with DEKA® transparent colors." Wigs for Rotraut Schrott studio dolls are custom crafted, often hand tied, and are made from European human hair. For finer-textured baby doll wigs, the artist uses mohair. Doll bodies are cotton calico stuffed with special batting.

Costumes for freely-designed artist dolls give Rotraut new opportunity for imaginative play. She has amassed a vast collection of precious antique fabrics, laces, trims, and accessory details over the years, and it is from this rich source that she draws when composing doll clothes enriched with lace, beads, feathers, and subtly-patterned century-old fabrics whose dyes have been reworked and softened by the mysterious forces of time. The clothing worn by commissioned portrait dolls, by contrast, corresponds line-for-line to contemporary garments actually worn by Rotraut's young sitters. And in at least one instance — a double portrait of brothers named Christoforo and Marcello — the 33in (84cm) dolls wear sailor suits borrowed from the boys' own bedroom closet!

"In the end, I don't think of my work as doll crafting," Rotraut said, "I 'create' children, as close to living boys and girls as my hands can make them. Which is why I so enjoy doing portrait dolls."

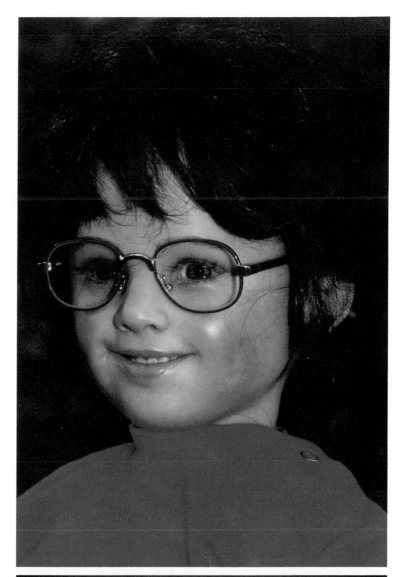

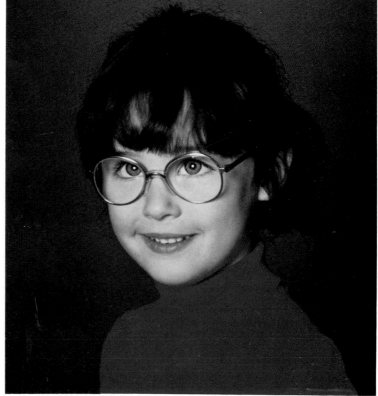

Top: A 1991 sculpted portrait of Christina, 32in (82cm) tall. Costumes for Rotraut's portrait dolls are designed directly from real clothing owned by her young models. Occasionally, her dolls wear actual garments from the subjects' wardrobes! *Photograph courtesy of Rotraut Schrott.*

Bottom: The real Christina who sat for the remarkable three-dimensional portrait shown. *Photograph courtesy of Rotraut Schrott.*

Like many contemporary German dollmakers, Rotraut Schrott enjoys the challenge of Third World children. Mario and Elena, shown here, are 33in (84cm) Peruvian siblings sculpted in 1992. *Photograph courtesy of Rotraut Schrott.*

Detail of Gina, shown on frontispiece.

A vinyl baby doll designed by Rotraut Schrott for GADCO® and issued as a numbered limited edition in 1993. *Photograph courtesy of Rotraut Schrott.*

Maxi, a slightly older and fairly sophisticated one-of-a-kind young lady sculpted in 1992, measures 30in (76cm) tall. *Photograph courtesy of Rotraut Schrott.*

Sisters, Julia (pink hat) and Laura (blue hat), a duo created in 1992. Note the attention to anatomy that gives life to the forms, the individuality of each girl, and the gorgeous use of color and texture in the execution of their costumes. *Photograph courtesy of Rotraut Schrott.*

Detail of previous illustration.

Beate Schult

"Making dolls gives me great pleasure," Beate Schult told the authors. "Through this craft, I can develop various interests and talents — form, color and originality." The wide-ranging career of this extraordinary Munich artist includes glass-painting, mosaic, painted canvases, graphic design, children's portraits, fashion design and sculpture, in addition to the *avant garde* dolls for which her studio is best known to contemporary collectors.

Beate Schult was born in the scenic Taunus Mountains district south of Frankfurt and studied glass-painting and mosaic art at the Craft School in Krefeld from 1961-1966. In 1961, at the tender age of 16, she became one of the youngest members of the Bayrischer Kunstgewerbe Verein (German Crafts Institute). From 1966-1970 she studied painting at the Academy of Plastic Arts in Nuremberg. She struck out on her own as an independent artist in 1971 and, that same year, she crafted her first artist dolls.

"When I was a child, I loved to play with dolls," Beate Schult told us. "While I was still a schoolgirl, I even made some dolls myself. But the first dolls I crafted as a professional artist were made in 1971 and were very small, close to dollhouse scale. These aroused considerable interest in the artist-doll marketplace."

Those first dolls were quickly followed by larger one-of-a-kind pieces, and by 1975 Beate Schult was crafting a variety of studio dolls in assorted sizes. The mood of those early dolls was romantic, nostalgic, — a unique blend of almost dainty prettiness with clean lines and powerful control of design elements and media. Head, arms, and legs for each were crafted in a wide range of materials; bodies were stuffed cloth. Beate styled each doll wig herself. She even made hats for her dolls, delightful creations in straw, ornamented with leaves and flowers. Subjects included boys and girls, theatrical personalities, even marionettes. Each doll was signed and dated on its left hand and not one, the artist said firmly, included prefabricated components or "found" accessories.

In 1985/1986, the artist made the first of the stunning leather dolls for which she has become famous. These dolls are deceptively traditional-looking. After all, much of the 19th-century's best doll art was crafted in leather. But there is no conscious attempt to be traditional here. Rather, these sturdy sheepskin or kidskin creations, which average 16in (40cm) tall, are experimental art, as is every product of Beate Schult's fertile studio. Each of her leather Children of The World is an attempt, the artist said, "to create through body design alone constructions in which nudity itself becomes an extraordinary form of clothing," a revelation of the soul as well as the personality of the subject. "My leather dolls are designed to be handled, to give tactile pleasure. They are made from top-quality, all-natural materials, and their bodies are purposely stylized and beautiful."

Stylized constructions that combine the human form with highly-experimental art are an important part of Beate Schult's studio work, and it's left to the collector, in the end, to determine which figures are dolls and which are not. "Each is an outgrowth of my fantasy," the artist said. "I adore experiments with different materials, to develop new techniques and explore new paths through my work."

A mixed media and fabric doll crafted in 1975. The artist even made the country straw hat worn by this 16in (40cm) beauty, whose features hint at the stylization and abstraction that increasingly characterize Beate Schult's work. *Photograph by Jörg Beske, Munich. Courtesy of Beate Schult.*

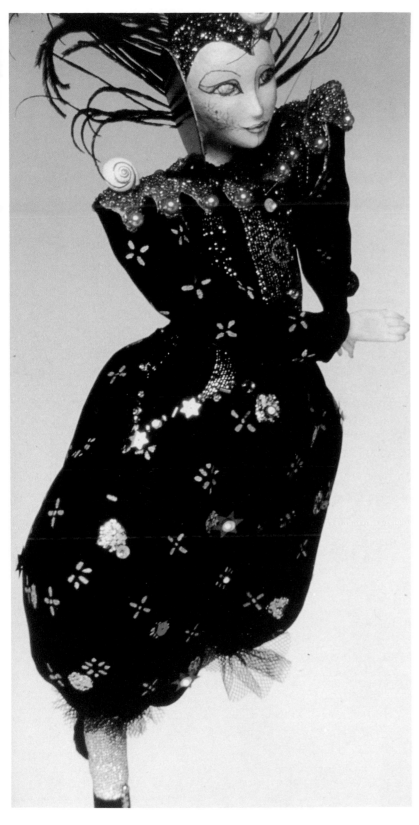

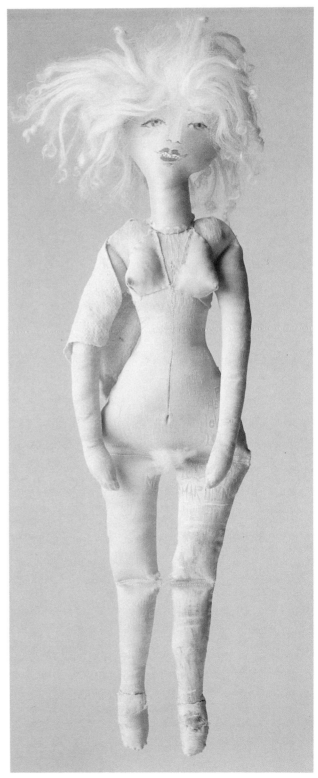

Dream Dancer, a 16in (40cm) mixed media and fabric doll crafted in 1984. Compare the doll with the straw hat (see page 132) to this fantasy *Traumtänzer* to understand the artist's increasingly abstract progression over a decade of studio work. Here, the Arabian Nights effect of the jewel-and-bead-encrusted costume, unseeing eyes, plumes, headdress, and the snails mesmerize the viewer. Nothing leads away from the surrealistic effect. *Photograph by Jörg Beske, Munich. Courtesy of Beate Schult.*

Marilyn, Beate Schult's painted-fabric, tongue-in-cheek bow to a famous personality, was crafted in 1987 and measures 13in (34cm) tall. Don't be fooled by the seeming simplicity of this piece. It is, in fact, a very complex, sophisticated piece of work. *Photograph by Jörg Beske, Munich. Courtesy of Beate Schult.*

133

Made in 1985, 18in (45cm) Struwwelmarie is a character invented by the artist to complement the famous boy of German children's literature, Struwwelpeter. Like Peter, Marie neglects her hair. Note the exquisitely painted features, the subtly-outlined lips and the delicately-feathered eyebrows. *Photograph by Jörg Beske, Munich. Courtesy of Beate Schult.*

Beate Schult's figures are made of painted fabric, wood-and-paper, steel wire, feathers, stones, — anything that will complete the artistic statement, contribute strength and meaning to the work-in-progress. "Belladonna" and two archangels illustrated here are visible demonstrations of the artist's fascinating but complex aesthetic. Each is a product of her private dream world; at the same time, it is a studied composition that combines elegant design elements, psychological tension, and an often-delightful innovative use of materials. In the group titled Belladonna, the painted-fabric sculptures tell their own amusing story. One wood-and-paper Archangel is a study in tension and tragedy. Cords bind the face and twist through the fierce lines of the crown. The other figure appears to be a messenger of peace. Archangel II balances delicately on a Plexiglas cube, its fragile wings constructed of feathers and dried lunaria seed pods.

Beate Schult dolls, like her paintings and sculptures, have evolved over the years and reflect the artist's ceaseless quest for techniques and materials through which to express a very private world of dreams. Composition, painted fabric, wood-and-paper, mixed media, kidskin, sheepskin — whatever material a Beate Schult doll is made from, it invariably reflects the dynamic experimental thrust and technical mastery that characterize work from this Munich studio.

Belladonna, crafted in 1988, is a trio of deceptively-primitive-looking painted fabric dolls. Each measures 13in (34cm) tall; together they form an amusing narrative. At left, the coy flirt; at center, the vain, disinterested young man; at right, the confident girlfriend. *Photograph by Jörg Beske, Munich. Courtesy of Beate Schult.*

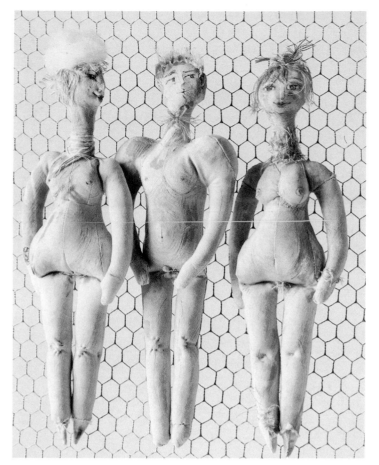

Archangel II, 12in (30cm) tall 1992 study, poised delicately on a Plexiglas cube. The piece has a theme of fragile beauty, brought home by the smooth surfaces and the use of natural materials, — feathers, dried lunaria — for the angel's wings. *Photograph by Jörg Beske, Munich. Courtesy of Beate Schult.*

Archangel crafted in 1991. The dynamism and muscle in this tension-laden paper, wood and cord composition suggest a scale and mass far greater than its diminutive 12in (30cm) size. *Photograph by Jörg Beske, Munich. Courtesy of Beate Schult.*

Detail of previous illustration. Tension and tragedy are evoked by the cords which bind the face of this Beate Schult Archangel. Note the symbolism of the cord interwoven with the spiky wooden crown. *Photograph by Jörg Beske, Munich. Courtesy of Beate Schult.*

Since 1985/1986, Beate Schult has developed a new type of doll, her Children of The World series crafted completely in leather. Of these *lederkinder* the artist says she "tries to create through body design constructions in which nudity itself becomes an extraordinary form of clothing" to reveal the personality and "soul" of the subject. *Photograph by Jörg Beske, Munich. Courtesy of Beate Schult.*

A group of *lederkinder* crafted in 1992. Children of The World dolls are made from sheepskin or kidskin. Some wear real fur wigs. *Photograph by Jörg Beske, Munich. Courtesy of Beate Schult.*

Elfriede Schwarzenbach-Weissenberger

"Dollmaking has been my hobby for over 20 years," explained Elfriede Schwarzenbach-Weissenberger, whose one-of-a-kind wood composition dolls are included in many of Europe's important collections. The artist, whose work influenced the evolving art of Sylvia Natterer, was herself inspired by the elegant composure that characterizes dolls by Swiss master artist Sasha Morgenthaler. "When my children were young," Elfriede said, "I was fascinated by Sasha Morgenthaler's dolls, but they were so expensive! I couldn't afford to buy them for my son and daughter, so I made dolls for them myself. Sasha Morgenthaler actually saw one of my first dolls and encouraged me to continue my studio efforts."

Elfriede Schwarzenbach was born in Hamburg in 1937, grew up in Munich, and has lived in Berne, Switzerland since 1961. As a young girl, she wanted to train for a career in the decorative or applied arts, but her father insisted that she enter the family printing business instead. Today, Elfriede works full-time as a photolithographer in Berne and the old dream persists. "If I'm able to give up this job one day," she mused, "I'd have more time for dolls. I look forward to the possibility with joy and considerable impatience. I've waited so long already. Perhaps I'd try my hand at porcelain and craft limited editions of special subjects."

Art is in Elfriede's blood! During a childhood lived in stark post-war Germany, she crafted her own toys, as few were available in shops. She taught herself to sculpt in wax and Plastillin®, to paint, and to work with paper. As a schoolgirl, she modelled heads for traditional Bavarian *Rauchgoldengels* (gold-tinselled angels) to decorate Christmas trees in her family's and her friends' homes. When, years later, this self-taught artist began to craft dolls for her own children, her work was quickly discovered by a decorative arts boutique near Gstaad. "The shop offered to market my dolls and provided the incentive to continue crafting them," she told the authors.

Beginning with Doll N°. 1, completed in 1970, each of Elfriede's children has an individually-sculpted wood composition head. Because the artist's original purpose was to craft affordable toys to be lugged about and loved by real boys and girls, early work (1970-1983) was "child-proof," with unbreakable stuffed-fabric hands and feet. In 1983, the artist first created display dolls for sophisticated adult collections — dolls with arms, legs and head sculpted from wood composition. This material air dries and requires no firing; finished components are refined and polished, then painted with acrylic colors. Doll eyes are usually painted although, very occasionally, Elfriede will use handblown glass eyes. Wigs, often cut and styled by the artist, are fashioned from a wide range of materials that includes human hair, hemp, mohair, fur, — anything in fact that will enhance the work of art and complete the visual statement. Doll bodies are sturdy cotton or tricot fabric sewn from the artist's original patterns, then stuffed with acrylic batting. Limbs are attached with disks and are posable.

Most of Elfriede's dolls are born within her imagination; some are inspired by paintings, photographs, folk or fairytales.

Icarus, the artist's rendering of the boy from the old Greek myth, combines the legendary bird-man costume with elements of Carnival! In the legend Icarus' feathered wings were glued with tar that melted when he flew too close to the sun. The boy plunged to his death in the sea which bears his name. Elfriede's Icarus is 18in (45cm) tall. *Photograph courtesy of Elfriede Schwarzenbach-Weissenberger.*

Detail of Icarus shown in previous illustration.

20in (50cm) one-of-a-kind girl doll with long hair. Colors for costumes are inspired by the tint and mood of a doll's hair and face. The artist designs her own patterns and hand sews all clothing from fine cotton or silk, often accented with delicate lengths of antique lace and ribbon. *Photograph courtesy of Elfriede Schwarzenbach-Weissenberger.*

This 14in (35cm) Girl with Short Hair is a study in brown and peach with subtle green accents. All dolls from this Berne studio are individually sculpted in wood composition. Features and eyes are painted with acrylic colors. Occasionally, Elfriede gives a doll handblown glass eyes. *Photograph courtesy of Elfriede Schwarzenbach-Weissenberger.*

A 16in (40cm) Swedish girl crafted in 1979 shows off the brightly-trimmed costume and sturdy red-and-white leather boots of her native province. This early piece dates from the time when Elfriede equated dolls with toys, — hence, the beautifully-detailed unbreakable cloth hands. Since 1983, the artist has sculpted arms and legs from wood composition. *Photograph courtesy of Elfriede Schwarzenbach-Weissenberger.*

Another 16in (40cm) doll with cloth hands and exquisitely-modelled wood composition features, this French country child was made in 1979. She wears a bright blue dress with a blue-and-white patterned apron. Note the high coloring, evidence of a life lived in the brisk outdoors of provincial France. *Photograph courtesy of Elfriede Schwarzenbach-Weissenberger.*

The subjects are invariably children. "I adore children," the artist declared enthusiastically. "To render as art the sweetness, solemnity, sorrow and merriment, all the nuances of expression that characterize faces of real children, — I find this fascinating. When I sculpt, I concentrate absolutely on the work-in-hand. Time and place are forgotten. And when a piece is finally completed, I am often more surprised than anyone else by the 'living being' my hands have created."

Fabric choice and colors for costumes are inspired by dolls' hair and eyes. Thus, Icarus, with his fierce bird mask and fantasy tunic overlaid with layers of rust, brown, gold and black feathers, has a mop of unruly honey-tone curls and liquid soft brown eyes. The Swedish girl doll from 1979 has short-cropped flaxen hair and blue-gray eyes. The bold blues and reds of her provincial dress and bonnet frame the face, while the cheerful trim, particularly the yellow rickrack, unifies the composition.

For Elfriede, however, the most important feature of any doll is its face. It is the face that provides the psychological link with the viewer, that establishes an empathetic bond or says nothing. "This factor is crucial," the artist told us. "A collector will only buy dolls with which she can fall in love."

Two young beauties crafted in 1990. Through clever costume and design detail, Elfriede has created contrasting personalities. The girl on the left, with her tiny teddy bear and somber outfit, complements her friend, who seems to personify fields, meadows, and the airy spirit of springtime. Both children are 16in (40cm) tall. *Photograph courtesy of Elfriede Schwarzenbach-Weissenberger.*

Detail of previous illustration.

Wiltrud Stein

"I love little things and always hope to craft small dolls 8in-12in (21cm-30cm) tall," artist Wiltrud Stein told the authors. "The great challenge for me," she added, "is to craft dolls that are as much as possible like real children, complete to the most subtle nuance of expression despite the constraints of their very small scale."

Wiltrud Stein has fond recollections of the one doll she possessed as a child. Because she wanted to provide an extensive and elaborate wardrobe for that doll, she studied and mastered a wide range of craft skills. She learned to sew and crochet at age nine, then tackled painting, pottery, sculpture, embroidery and knitting. "With scraps of fabric, I created a complete trousseau for my doll," she told us. "My design source was patterns used for my own full-size dresses." Several years later, Wiltrud tried her hand at cloth dollmaking, using a biology textbook as a guide for the correct human proportions. "For a while, my friends and family received lots of rag dolls as gifts," she said.

Despite Wiltrud's evident talent for handcrafts and the arts, her parents urged her to pursue a career in commerce. She

was destined for an artist's life, however, and had few regrets when an early marriage ended the commercial career almost before it began. In her new home, she transformed a corner of the basement into a complete workshop, a magic studio where she designed and sewed clothing for herself and her two children. Wiltrud made stuffed animals, marionettes, rocking horses, and dollhouses complete with in-scale furniture. She took classes in cabinet-making, and during an advanced pottery course had the idea to sculpt dolls, working from photographs of children she knew well. In an article published a decade later in the *Magazine de la Maison de Poupée*," author Sylvie Narrat describes the artist's first studio doll, an effort which impressed her classmates but failed to satisfy her own perfectionist standards. Wiltrud jammed Doll #1 back into the clay barrel.

Luckily for the collecting world, Wiltrud Stein continued her dollmaking experiments. It wasn't long before the artist's work was coveted by European collectors. Early in her career, Wiltrud won second prize in an amateur dollmaking contest and, in 1990, she won one silver and two gold medals

Franziska, a one-of-a-kind 8in (21cm) Sleeping Baby made in 1992. Wiltrud's babies fit in the palm of one's hand, where they wiggle and snuggle into the coziest positions! *Photograph courtesy of Wiltrud Stein.*

A 12in (30cm) one-of-a-kind Eskimo girl. "Before I actually begin sculpting a new piece, I have the design complete in my imagination," Wiltrud said. This small Native American won a ribbon in San Mateo, California in 1990. *Photograph courtesy of Wiltrud Stein.*

This 12in (30cm) one-of-a-kind Oriental girl has a mohair wig cut and styled by the artist. Wiltrud designs all clothing, including undergarments, worn by her dolls. For one-of-a-kind pieces, she also sews the costumes, knits caps and sweaters, and crochets tiny booties. Limited-edition dolls wear outfits crafted by studio assistants who work from the artist's original patterns. *Photograph courtesy of Wiltrud Stein.*

at an International Show and Competition in Berne, Switzerland. That same year, she won a ribbon at San Mateo, California for her little Eskimo girl and, in 1991, yet another ribbon for one of her adorable sleeping babies.

One of the charms of dollmaking for an artist like Wiltrud Stein is the way the field integrates a wide spectrum of craft skills. The daily routine in the studio demands expertise in sculpting, designing, knitting, crocheting, sewing, embroidery, and painting. Plaster molds must be constructed from clay prototypes; porcelain slip must be poured; fragile greenware must be smoothed and refined. The tasks are endless and, for Wiltrud, the variety is part of what makes the art so exciting.

Mastery of the technical side of dollmaking frees the artist to express her inner self, and for Wiltrud this means power to explore the many faces of childhood. "I have always loved to observe young children," she confided. "Their gestures and body language reveal their sensitivity. Older children and adults manage to mask their feelings, but children under

six are an open book, and the possibilities for the artist are nearly infinite."

It is one thing to recognize the infinite variety and beauty of childhood. It is quite another to depict it as three-dimensional art, and Wiltrud worked hard to develop the skill. "At first I struggled to reproduce live models in the most precise detail possible. Later, I found that my dolls were a reflection of my own state of mind, not that of the children I was rendering. Today," Wiltrud said, "my dolls have finally become artistic creations with lives of their own."

Before Wiltrud Stein crafts a one-of-a-kind doll or the prototype for a limited edition of 10-25, she "sees" the work of art complete to the last detail in her mind's eye. Once the image is fixed, she sculpts the doll's head in clay, takes a mold from the prototype and reproduces the face in porcelain. If the porcelain head is identical to the imagined one, she completes the project. If not, she destroys the head and begins again.

A one-of-a-kind Indian boy wears a bold black-and-white sweatshirt designed by the artist. The illusion of energetic, pulsing life is extraordinary when one realizes the wee lad measures a scant 12in (30cm) tall. *Photograph courtesy of Wiltrud Stein.*

A plump girlfriend for Wiltrud's Indian boy! The purposeful selection of fabric, texture and color enhances the warm tones of the child's complexion, rich black hair, and intense dark eyes. The turquoise barrette adds an exquisite finishing touch to this one-of-a-kind composition. *Photograph courtesy of Wiltrud Stein.*

Each Wiltrud Stein doll has a porcelain head, arms and legs. Features, including eyes, are painted with waterbase colors. Babies are stuffed with granules which add weight to the dolls and give the illusion that adorable 8in (21cm) infants are actually snuggling deep into the hands that hold them. Older child dolls (2-6 year olds) have wire-armature skeletons filled with acrylic batting. Before 1992, one-of-a-kind dolls had real kidskin bodies; since that year, one-of-a-kinds, like Wiltrud's limited-edition series dolls, have bodies crafted from sturdy cotton. Wigs are hand tied, then cut and styled by the artist, using fine mohair which is, she believes, scaled right for small dolls. "Human hair is too coarse for such little children," Wiltrud said.

Every Wiltrud Stein doll costume is a unique design by the artist. Fabrics are natural fiber. Real leather shoes are handcrafted to her specifications by a professional dolls' shoemaker. She personally sews clothing, knits sweaters, caps and baby booties, and crafts all accessories for her one-of-a-kind dolls. Studio helpers dress series dolls, working from prototypes completed by the artist. It is sometimes hard to locate suitable fabrics with patterns small enough to suit Wiltrud's little people, but the search is part of the fun and she enjoys it.

When Wiltrud Stein thinks back to her own childhood, she regrets that she had only one doll. "My dream of owning a Käthe Kruse doll has remained a dream to this day," she said ruefully. "When my daughter was old enough for dolls, I made sure she had the loveliest I could find in the shops." One wonders whether Wiltrud's little girl might have preferred a few samples from her own mother's studio!

Whatever these one-of-a-kind Wiltrud Stein children are discussing, it's clearly not meant for our ears! The 12in (30cm) boy and girl are sculpted, assembled, and costumed from the skin outward by the artist. Doll shoes are made to her specifications by a dolls' shoemaker. *Photograph courtesy of Wiltrud Stein.*

A 1992 limited edition of 12, this 12in (30cm) youngster has a face that combines charm with stubbornness. *Photograph courtesy of Wiltrud Stein.*

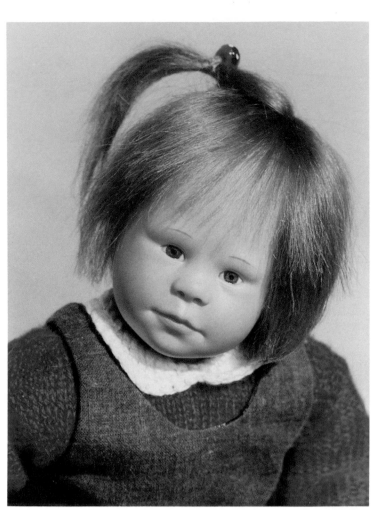

Eve, an impish porcelain toddler 10in (25cm) long, was crafted in 1993. *Photograph courtesy of Wiltrud Stein.*

Sabrina was a 1993 special edition of 20 created for the Paris-based C.F.P.A.C. (Club Français de la Poupée d'Artiste et Contemporaine). Sabrina is 8in (21cm) long. *Photograph courtesy of Wiltrud Stein.*

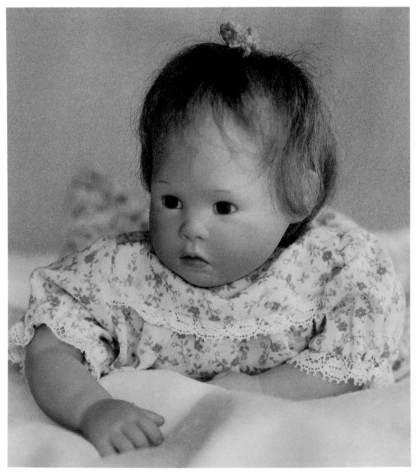

A lovable 8in (21cm) Chinese baby, all the more adorable because his richly-colored suit is slightly oversized. How vulnerable he appears, seated alone on such a great big blanket! *Photograph courtesy of Wiltrud Stein.*

Author Ann Bahar is mother to a pair of active twins and remembers scenes like the one pictured here. In infant logic, the quickest route between two points is *always* a straight line, even when it means crawling over a sibling! *Photograph courtesy of Wiltrud Stein.*

Another view of the previous illustration.

Katharina, a 32in (81cm) one-of-a-kind porcelain doll, relaxes and daydreams in a doll-size porch chair. Katharina's filmy old-fashioned dress with its lovely lace inserts, her straw hat with its fabric flowers and streamers, and the backdrop — a hint of summer gardens and lattice trellises — all contribute to the mood and concentrate our understanding of the doll's inner life. *Photograph courtesy of Ruth Treffeisen.*

Detail of the previous illustration.

Ingrid Winter

"I owe an enormous debt to Barbie®. Without her, I certainly wouldn't be a dollmaker today," declares artist Ingrid Winter, whose love of dolls and training in crafts grew out of a childhood world in which Barbie® dolls were definitely center stage. "I had 17 Barbies® which I've kept over the years and occasionally bring out for old-time's sake on rainy days," Ingrid explained. "A doll family that big needs lots of clothes, and since the Barbie® doll manufacturer's wardrobes were priced beyond my schoolgirl purse — and since birthdays and Christmas never came round fast enough to satisfy me — I began crafting dolls' clothes myself. At first I just glued bits of fabric together, but a family friend soon took me in hand and taught me the proper way to use needle and thread."

The friend who taught Ingrid basic sewing skills still recalls, 25 years later, the seriousness of that little pupil and how stubbornly she worked to master the seamstress's art. In the child's mind, of course, the exquisite small garments she

Ingrid Winter is especially fond of 30in (75cm) one-of-a-kind Enya crafted in 1989. Enya's head and limbs are molded white porcelain; her body is stuffed fabric constructed around a sturdy wire armature. For this doll's wig, the artist used her own hair, painstakingly inset one hair at a time into the wax coating that overlays the porcelain head. *Photograph by Volker Wengert. Courtesy of Ingrid Winter.*

was learning to design and assemble weren't doll clothes; they were clothes for real little people, for small-scale, beloved playmates whose lives she shared inside a secret play world. The pattern of that personal childhood world, with its fusion of play and the creative process, defines the soul of the artist for dollmaker Ingrid Winter. "I believe the artist absorbs real-life experience and associations, that these then recombine with the artist's imagination, like patterns in a kaleidoscope, to emerge as new realities within the arts," she said.

During her teens, when peers put aside the toys of childhood, Ingrid discovered how deeply attached she was to her dolls. "I would have considered it betrayal of dear friends to banish my Barbies®," she said. "One day, I knew, I would have to turn my back on childhood, but in the meantime I kept my private world alive in secret.

The need to choose a practical career track led Ingrid to a degree program in fashion design where she studied graphics and mastered the subtleties of dress design and pattern construction, but the logical outcome of her studies, a career in the fashion advertising industry, was hardly inspiring. She needed freedom, to be able to create from within herself.

Then, in 1982, the artist met Brigitte Lohrmann, whose shop in Hamburg was among the first in Europe to showcase contemporary artist dolls. Brigitte Lohrmann's shop opened the door to the future for Ingrid Winter. It provided a gallery full of first-rate doll art by top artists to learn from and study. Mrs. Lohrmann was able to direct Ingrid to supply sources for materials and dolls for porcelain dollmaking. "After the lucky meeting with Brigitte Lohrmann in 1982," Ingrid told the authors, "I became completely dedicated to the dollmaker's art."

Each one-of-a-kind Ingrid Winter doll begins as a rough clay sculpture from which the artist designs an even rougher mold. The real work comes when the poured porcelain emerges from the mold. Ingrid devotes long hours to sculpting fine detail and refining each piece until even work formed within the same mold takes on the quality and uniqueness of one-of-a-kind doll art.

"I love the elegant glow of fine porcelain," the artist told us, "and I try, through sculpted detail and painting, to enrich and warm this essentially cold medium." She mixes her own colors and applies delicate layers of paint, much as an artist working in two dimensions builds color and texture on a fine canvas. For each doll, she decides whether painted or inset glass eyes best suit the artistic statement.

Ingrid designs and personally sews each costume worn by her dolls which range from storybook characters to sensitive portrait dolls and figures of purest fantasy. Their clothes, fashioned from fabrics and trims garnered during decades of collecting, include old and new velvets, silks, leathers, and furs, precious laces and gold braids, antique buttons, beads, sequins, silk flowers, feathers, and more. "I don't craft *doll* costumes," the artist explained. "I craft real clothing in miniature, with the linings, insertions, and closures one finds in the *haute couture* of the real world."

Large dolls from this studio average 26in-30in (65cm-75cm) tall and have human hair wigs. (The artist also crafts miniature dolls which have mohair wigs.) Doll bodies are usually linen or cotton, well stuffed and built around a posable wire armature. Beginning in 1992, Ingrid has experimented with static porcelain costumed figures in addition to her elegant posable dolls. These add dimension to the artist's power of expression and provide a new challenge, and challenge is what Ingrid Winter seems to enjoy most.

Le Lis (The Lily) is a 28in (70cm) white porcelain doll with glass eyes and a human hair wig elegantly styled by the artist. Lily's dress is cotton batiste and silk. "I do not make *doll* clothes," the artist said emphatically. "I craft real outfits in miniature, complete to the finest dressmaking detail. *Photograph by Volker Wengert. Courtesy of Ingrid Winter.*

Romeo and Juliet, 26in (65cm) and 24in (62cm) respectively, are a one-of-a-kind duet delicately painted and exquisitely costumed. Note the attention to period costume and to the Renaissance contour and coloration of Juliet's face. Both dolls have painted eyes and lashes. Romeo's wig is sheepwool; Juliet has a human hair wig. *Photograph courtesy of Ingrid Winter.*

Salome is a one-of-a-kind doll crafted entirely from white bisque. The 28in (70cm) figure, created in 1992, has a human hair wig, glass eyes, and real hair lashes. Her exotic artist-designed and crafted costume is fine silk. *Photograph courtesy of Ingrid Winter.*

An exquisite one-of-a-kind miniature clown bust crafted in 1992. Observe how asymmetrical painted detail heightens the power of the design. *Photograph courtesy of Ingrid Winter.*

One-of-a-kind Alice in Wonderland doll crafted in 1990. This 26in (65cm) interpretation of a beloved theme gazes, amazed, at the unexpected sights "down the rabbit hole." The artist's charming interpretation of Lewis Carroll's White Rabbit holds the watch from its waistcoat pocket. *Photograph courtesy of Ingrid Winter.*

A one-of-a-kind portrait doll sculpted in 1992. Eyes and lips are so expressive it is difficult to conceive that this beautiful child is cold porcelain! *Photograph courtesy of Ingrid Winter.*

Claudia Zufferey-Mayer

"I'm living proof that one can craft marionettes without having felt a special empathy for dolls during childhood," artist Claudia Zufferey-Mayer told the authors, with a mischievous grin. "When I was a girl, I put my dolls to bed each night — not under the covers, but rather under the mattress! And when my parents gave a 'first doll' to my sisters and me, I removed its arms and legs so we could share the present equitably among the three of us."

As a school girl, this dynamic artist was passionately interested in drawing and was often scolded for inattention to lessons, particularly in French and Math classes. "I also recall how, during my teens, I tried to make sense of the mysterious world of three dimensions," Claudia told us. "With money earned during summer vacations, I bought clay and modelled my first figures." During those years, Claudia's

The artist conceives of her exotic marionettes as mannequins capable of taking all sorts of beautiful poses. Frequently, a choice bit of fabric will inspire an entire project, including the tone of the make-up worn by the puppet. *Photograph courtesy of Claudia Zufferey-Mayer.*

mother taught her sewing skills and appreciation of the special pleasure that comes with a job well done. When the young artist realized she could fuse her interests by becoming a fashion designer, she was elated. But her more practical parents advised that she train for work as a licensed paramedic, a career track they knew would provide steady employment, something that has never been guaranteed in the studio arts.

Fortunately for collectors around the world (Claudia Zufferey-Mayer's marionettes figure in collections in Europe, the United States, Taiwan and Japan), the practical side of earning a living failed to dampen her enthusiasm for fashion design, drawing, and sculpture. Eventually, she was introduced to the marionette theatre through the work of her sister, Sylvia Natterer (see page 88). Claudia was quick to join Sylvia's troupe and, she explained joyously, "When I dressed those wonderful small 'people', when I designed their costumes, everything came together; I realized my childhood dream. It was that simple."

The artist's fascination with the construction rather than the animation of marionettes led to her first original creation, the geographer from Antoine de Saint-Exupéry's classic tale, *The Little Prince.* A second marionette, which was exhibited in a group show at the Musée des Arts Décoratifs at Lausanne in 1977, gave Claudia her first view of the vast spectrum of contemporary doll artistry and provided inspiration to continue in the field. And when one of her own marionettes placed second among 500 entrants in a 1980 International Doll Competition at Zurich, her future was sealed. "Without the Zurich prize, I might not have dared to take the step that transformed a childhood dream into a 15-year passion," the artist said. "And I would have missed the pleasure of seeing my marionettes become part of important collections around the world."

Claudia's marionettes aren't numbered because the artist only crafts one-of-a-kind pieces. Sizes vary from figure to figure, but all have stuffed fabric bodies with limbs and faces sculpted from wood composition. Wood composition components are sanded, then painted with gouache or watercolor. Claudia purposely applies heavy makeup to her marionettes' faces and crowns their heads with elaborate, often fantastic, turbans. Colors for makeup, — indeed the entire thrust of a design — may be inspired by a choice bit of rare cloth, a length of irridescent silk, a gorgeous gold-embroidered fragment.

For Claudia Zufferey-Mayer, the most important aspect of any project is the facial expression and the elegant, long-fingered hands of a marionette. Through her art she strives to define the feminine mystique. Thus, purity of line is more important than realistic depiction of human features and proportions. "For me, the marionettes are wired dolls," she explained. "They are mannequins capable of assuming a wide range of lifelike poses to show their beautiful costumes to optimal advantage. It takes a long time to craft a single one-of-a-kind piece. I work without sketches; I plunge directly

Detail of illustration on previous page.

Most marionettes from this Swiss-based studio wear turbans rather than wigs. When a particular piece requires a wig to complete the statement, Claudia proves herself master of the wigmaker's art, as evidenced by the blond confection sported by this exotic harpist. *Photograph courtesy of Claudia Zufferey-Mayer.*

Claudia found her true profession when she encountered the marionette troupe established by her sister, artist Sylvia Natterer (see page 88). The medium permitted a fusion of her three passions: drawing and design, fabrics and textiles, and fashion design. *Photograph courtesy of Claudia Zufferey-Mayer.*

This sophisticated marionette, with her elongated hands, magnificently detailed turban, and heavily painted face, is a typical statement by the artist, whose one-of-a-kind figures nearly always evoke the feminine mystique. *Photograph courtesy of Claudia Zufferey-Mayer.*

into my medium. In general, I craft a number of marionettes at the same time. I sculpt, erase, redo, until each acquires an expressive power that touches it with humanness, with femininity."

This artist feels no deep attachment to her work once it is completed; she experiences few regrets when finished marionettes leave the studio to take up residence in private or museum collections. Collectors will be interested to learn that

this gifted lady, whose one-of-a-kind pieces are rare prizes, contracted with the German firm, GÖTZ, in 1992, to design a marionette for commercial manufacture. The piece initiates a series called "Coco's Fashion Stage" and will showcase the evolution of 20th century feminine costume. For her studio work, however, Claudia feels special kinship with the 1920s. "My marionettes are, above all else, decorative personalities," she said. "They are mannequins escaped from the Belle Epoque where *art deco* was king."

Christiane Besch

Artist Signature: Prior to 1992, all dolls were signed "Be", with the signature positioned high on the upper back. Starting in 1992, the signature includes the year of manufacture (see below) appearing on the neck, just below the base of the wig.

Be
92

Changes over Time: In 1992, Christiane Besch began crafting child dolls as well as historic adult fashion dolls. She is fascinated by the contrast between old and young faces, "old faces that look back into the past, young faces turned toward the future." She plans to design groups that combine old and young, grandparents and grandchildren, to add dimension and poetry to her work.

Doll Sizes: Adult dolls average 20in (50cm) tall. Child dolls average 12in (31cm) tall.

Work with Industry: As of June 1992, Christiane Besch had never contracted to work with industry.

Sale of Molds: As of June 1992, the artist had not sold her molds for use by amateurs.

Rolanda Heimer

Artist Signature: Each one-of-a-kind doll is marked on the neck or behind the ear with an RH:

Changes Over Time: "I began with caricature dolls in 1983. The caricature element was subdued as I moved forward to 'old people dolls'," Rolanda said. "Newborns and children are my most recent additions. I have so many ideas; it's quite possible that my dolls will continue to evolve in the future."

Work with Industry: As of February 1992, Rolanda Heimer has never worked with a manufacturer. She told us she doubts she ever will. "I don't want to lose my freedom!"

Sale of Molds: This artist has not sold her designs. She has no molds, since each individual doll is sculpted directly in clay.

Artist Signature: One-of-a-kind dolls are signed with the studio name, last names of the artists, the word *unikat* (one-of-a-kind), and the year; series dolls bear the studio name, series number, name of the doll, and the year (see below).

*Heiri
Buresch-Psotka
unikat 19 ....*

*Heiri Serie 92
Heiro " 25/25
1992*

Changes over Time: "Our dolls are always evolving. The only constant is our use of porcelain," said artists Iris Buresch and Heide Psotka. "Until 1991, our doll heads were mounted on conventional shoulderplates. Since 1992, they have full molded-porcelain busts."

Also in 1992, Heiri-Puppen presented its first two series dolls at the Nuremberg Toy Fair. In that year, the artists told us they prefer to sculpt directly in porcelain and were undecided about whether they would craft other limited edition dolls in future.

Doll Sizes: Sizes have varied over time. In 1992, one-of-a-kind baby dolls measured 12in (30cm), 16in (40cm), 18in (47cm) and 26in (65cm). One-of-a-kind child dolls were 24in (60cm) and 32in (80cm). Series dolls were 20in (50cm) tall.

Work with Industry/Sale of Molds: The artists do neither, since they believe a bond exists between the craftsman and the doll and that this is the essence of a doll's integrity. They do teach dollmaking classes, and they have authored two books for amateur dollmakers.

Annette Himstedt

Changes over Time: "I am constantly changing the shape and overall expression of my dolls. Today, I model babies, children and adults," the artist told us in 1992.

Work with Industry: Annette Himstedt's porcelain dolls are manufactured in the artist's home town of Paderborn, Germany, in the artist's private factory. Her vinyl dolls have been produced in a Spanish factory since 1986. Annette does not own this factory, but she set it up herself and it is the sole producer of her vinyl dolls.

Annette Himstedt vinyl doll issues through 1994:

1986/1987	Bastian	1990/1991	Fiene
	Ellen		Mo
	Käthe		Taki
	Paula		Ännchen
	Lisa		
	Fatou	1991/1992	Shireem
	Bekus		Liliane
			Neblina
1987/1988	Toni		
	Timi	1992/1993	Jule
			Enzo
1988/1989	Michiko		Sanga
	Makimura		Pemba
	Malin		
	Friederike	1993/1994	Lona
	Kasimir		Tara
			Kima
1989/1990	Janka		
	Adrienne		
	Ayoka		
	Kai		

Artist Signature: The following is engraved on the back of each doll's head: "Original, Annette Himstedt, Kinder aus Porzellan, made in Paderborn, Germany, the doll's name and number." Also the logo shown below.

Sale of Molds: "I have never sold my molds and will not do so in the future," the artist said.

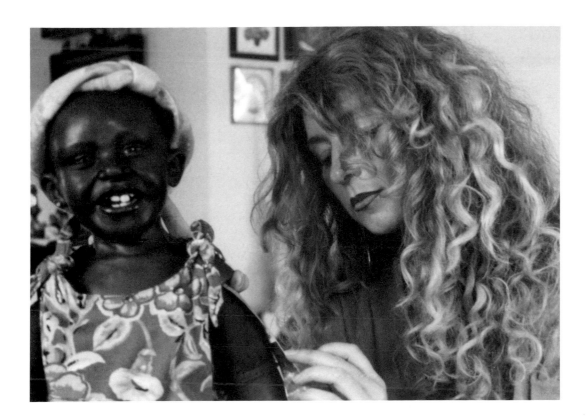

Artist Signature: Every Renate Hornung doll bears the artist's initials (see below), the month and year of completion on the reverse of the sculpted shoulders.

Changes over Time: There have been many small changes as the artist's work evolved. She considers the most important change to be her decision, in 1991, to sculpt each head and bust as a single unit. Before that year, Renate Hornung's dolls had movable heads inset into separately-crafted busts. The visible neck joint disturbed her, hence the 1991 refinement in her designs.

Doll Sizes: The artist told us in 1992 that all her dolls measure between 32in (80cm) - 34in (85cm) tall, with the exception of occasional specially-commissioned smaller dolls. Starting in 1993, all Renate Hornung dolls measure 28in (70cm) tall.

Jutta Kissling

Artist Signature: Each doll is signed (see below) at the back of the neck and marked with the year of manufacture as well as a letter code to indicate the original sculpted head used for the edition.

Certificate: Each doll is accompanied by a signed, dated certificate from the artist, which includes the name and series number of the doll (see illustration).

Work With Industry: As of February 1992, Jutta Kissling has never accepted a commission from a manufacturer. "Through reproduction in quantity, regardless of the material used, the quality of dolls invariably suffers," she told us.

Sale of Molds: This artist has not sold any of her original molds for use by amateurs.

Certificate	Zertifikat
I hereby certify, that this doll	Ich bestätige hiermit, daß die Puppe
	VERA 5/15/1989
is designed and fully handmade by me.	von mir entworfen und hergestellt wurde.
The body is completely made of fine biscuit porcelain. The wig is human hair/best quality mohair. The clothing is made of natural materials, the shoes of real leather.	Der gesamte Körper ist aus Biscuit - Porzellan, die Perücke aus Echthaar/ bestem Mohair, die Kleidung aus Natur- stoffen, die Schuhe aus echtem Leder.
The doll is signed by me on the neck. The edition is limited to 15.	Die Puppe ist im Nacken signiert. Die limitierte Auflage beträgt 15 Stück.

München 1989

Maria Luise Lehner-von Lemcke

Artist Signature: During the 1980s, Frau von Lemcke attached one of the labels pictured here to each of her dolls. Today, each doll is signed at the back of the neck just below the wig. Signature includes the artist's initials, year, and name of the doll (MvL 91 Ronja).

Stylistic Changes over Time: Earliest dolls had cloth faces, but the artist soon graduated to air-drying clay, trade name DAS-PRONTO®. Since 1983, dolls have glass rather than painted eyes. Since 1989, arms and legs for one-of-a-kind dolls have been sculpted from FIMO®. Before 1989 they were cloth.

Doll Sizes: Dolls from this studio range from 12-22in (30-55cm) and include limited editions in ceramic and porcelain as well as one-of-a-kind pieces crafted from DAS-PRONTO®, the artist's favorite air-drying clay.

Work with Industry: In 1983, Brigitte Lohrmann was licensed to manufacture two dolls designed by Maria Luise Lehner-von Lemcke, — a 14in (35cm) doll with a porcelain head and a 20in (50cm) doll in vinyl.

In 1985, Mme. A.M. Rothkirch-Holzer was licensed to produce vinyl dolls from Lehner-von Lemcke designs.

Elisabeth Lindner

Changes Over Time: "Since 1991, I give my dolls lower-lid eyelashes as well as lashes on upper lids. Painted features of recent work are softer and more natural-looking than on my earlier pieces," Elisabeth Lindner said.

Work With Industry: Since 1993, Elisabeth Lindner had designed vinyl dolls manufactured by GÖTZ. The first group of three dolls included a boy, girl and baby.

Sale of Molds: Since 1991, Elisabeth has created two molds per year for sale to collectors and hobbyists. These molds are stamped with her studio address, the mold number and the artist's studio name, "LISON".

The above molds are never used by the artist; they are for use by amateurs only. Elisabeth notes that components differ from molds for her professional dollmaking. "For the molds which I sell, doll legs are sculpted to the knees, arms to the elbows. In my professional studio, legs and arms are complete and cast in white china."

Note: Collectors may know this artist by her former name, Elisabeth Özdemir.

Artist Signature: Each Lindner doll is marked in paint with the year of production and the series number. Each doll also wears a "gold" bracelet inscribed with the doll's name. The artist's studio name, "LISON", (see below) is engraved on the back of each doll head.

Artist Signature: "I sign my dolls with the first letters of my name and the year. Sometimes I add the doll's name," said Gabriele Lipp. "Sometimes I forget to sign a doll, but I can always recognize my own artwork. When I began making dolls, signatures were printed; today I use cursive."

Changes over Time: Gabriele Lipp's early dolls lacked ears; hands were mitten shapes without fingers. Hair was wool or flax. Little by little, the artist's needlesculpture and costuming became more refined and sophisticated and increasingly detailed. While early dolls looked very much alike, today each is a distinct personality.

Work with Industry: "My dolls don't lend themselves to commercialization," the artist said. "Each is a one-of-a-kind work of art."

A

Sylvia Natterer

Artist Signature: Sylvia Natterer dolls have always been signed at the back of the head and neck. Starting in 1990, the artist has also incised her name in full, along with the name of the doll. (See diagram.)

Stylistic Changes Over Time: Early Natterer dolls were made exclusively of wood composition with stuffed cloth bodies and legs. Since 1982, her dolls are porcelain, with porcelain arms and legs. Also in 1982, Sylvia crafted her first baby doll, with a stockinette body and hands, legs and head of porcelain. Today, the artist's infant dolls have porcelain legs, arms and head.

Work With Industry: Since 1989, Sylvia Natterer has worked with GÖTZ of Rodertal, Germany. Using the artist's prototypes, GÖTZ manufactures dolls for children under the trade name *Fanouche et ses amis*.

For the Franklin Mint (USA) in 1990, Sylvia designed a series of seven dolls each 9in (23cm) tall, to represent the seven days of the week. The dolls are porcelain, manufactured in Malaysia, and are not meant to be collector quality.

Sale of Molds: Sylvia Natterer does not sell her molds for use by amateurs.

Artist Signature: Each doll is signed on the soles of both feet (see below) with the artist's name, the name of the doll, the year and the series number.

Doll Size: Tamara Neumann dolls average 8in (20cm) tall.

Stylistic Changes Over Time: "I have made no significant changes since I began crafting my dolls," the artist told us in 1992.

Work with Industry: Tamara has been approached by mega firms, but as of 1992 had not contracted to design dolls to be issued by them in large series. She feels that the value of her work is its individuality and the fact that each doll is, from start to finish, meticulously crafted by the artist in her own studio.

Sale of Molds: It is our understanding that Tamara Neumann has not sold her molds for use by amateurs.

Elisabeth Pongatz

Photograph by John Gould, London, Courtesy of Elisabeth Pongratz.

Artist Signature: Dolls are signed with a distinctive grey logo, either on the left foot or at the center of the back. Three versions of the logo are shown below: (1) before March 1990; (2) since March 1990; (3) logo of the New Munich Art Dolls Co. based in Virginia, USA.

(1)

(2)

(3)

Changes over Time: Elisabeth first experimented with cloth and clay, then elected to use wood as the medium for her doll art. She has crafted all-wooden dolls and dolls with wooden heads and cloth bodies and limbs since the early 1980s. Sizes and materials have remained constant.

Doll Sizes: All-wood child dolls are 14in (36cm) and 10in (24cm) tall. Child dolls with wooden heads and cloth bodies measure 15in (38cm) and 10in (25cm). Babies are available in three sizes: 7in (18cm), 10in (25cm) and 12in (30cm).

Work with Industry: Since 1991-1992, Elisabeth Pongratz has worked with her friend Rhonda Weinstein to produce affordable dolls for children. Rhonda's firm, based in Virginia, USA, is called the New Munich Art Dolls Co. and is licensed by Dr. and Mrs. Pongratz to produce dolls as a cottage industry, working from designs and a prototype head supplied by the artist. New Munich Art Dolls Co. girl and boy dolls are signed with the name of the firm and the year; they also wear tags bearing the firm name.

Artist Signature: Dolls are signed on the back of the head with the artist's name, name of the doll, number of the doll, number of the month, and the year. Example:

Cara-Puppe		Carla Rauser
17-2/91	or	**17-2/91**
Manuela		**Manuela**

Changes Over Time: "Over the years, my basic style has remained the same, but the dolls keep improving," the artist said. "I continually sculpt new arms and legs and each time I realize an improvement over previous models, I discard the old molds."

Work With Industry: Since 1990, Carla Rauser has designed limited-edition porcelain dolls for SIGIKID®. Heads and shoulderplates are crafted and painted by the artist who also insets the doll's crystal eyes. SIGIKID® adds bodies, wigs and costumes. These dolls are sold through various outlets, including the annual Nuremberg Toy Fair.

Sale of Molds: As of May 1992, the artist had not sold any of her molds and had no plans to do so in the future.

Regina & Abhinavo Sandreuter

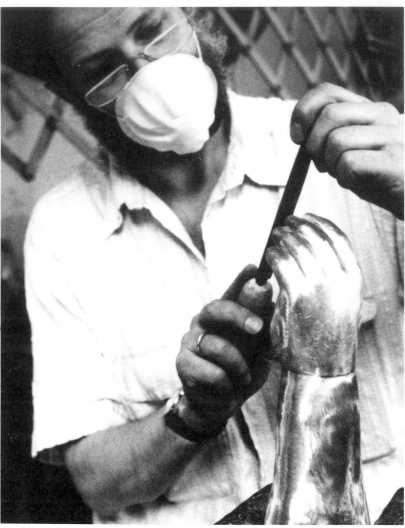

Artist Signature: Regina and Abhinavo Sandreuter's dolls are signed at the back of the neck with the artists' monogram framed by a copyright stamp.

Until late 1985, the monogram was:

Since 1985, the monogram has been:

Stylistic Changes Over Time: "We have always tried to improve our dolls according to our ideas of what they should be like," Regina explained. "So far, the moment we mastered one process we found ourselves facing a new challenge. Yet after 10 years of dollmaking, we increasingly feel the physical strain that comes with intensive work. Our eyes and hands, in particular, show signs of wear, and we wonder what and how much we will be able to do in the future."

The Sandreuters have used different materials for their dolls over the years:

1981-1986	resin dolls
Since 1986	wooden dolls with 8-part wooden body
Since 1990	wooden dolls with 12-part wooden (MultiPose) body
Beginning 1992	porcelain dolls with 12-part porcelain body

Work with Industry: Up to the time of our interview, the Sandreuters had not worked with industry.

Sale of Molds: "We have never given or sold heads, molds or parts to anybody," Regina said. "Our resin dolls, to our knowledge, have been copied twice, but the copies were poor quality and did not include our monogram or name."

Artist Signature: Signature and year are entered on one-of-a-kind dolls. (See below) Series dolls are signed, dated, and marked. Example: 101/30-1 where 101 is the series number, 30 the number of pieces in the series, and 1 indicates the number of the doll within the series.

Stylistic Changes over Time: "Over the years, my dolls have become more detailed, more realistic," said artist Karin Schmidt. "At the end of 1991, I crafted three dolls, each a limited edition of 30. While these were my first series dolls, I plan to continue making one-of-a-kinds as well."

Work With Industry: "In 1992 I was represented at the New York Toy Fair by DOLLMAKERS ORIGINALS. This was my first real link with industry," she said. In 1993, Karin released her first dolls for GÖTZ, three models in porcelain in limited editions of 100 each, and several dolls in vinyl.

Sale of Molds: The artist has never sold her molds.

Vera Scholz

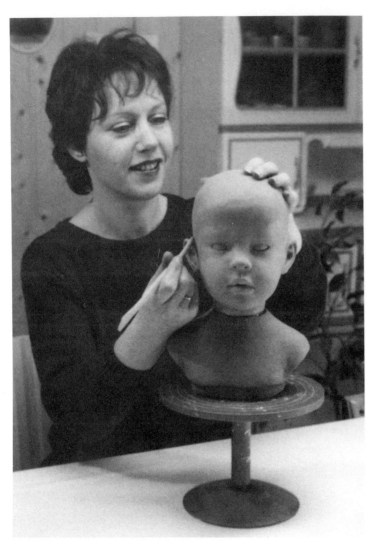

Artist Signature: Each Vera Scholz doll is marked on the back of the neck with the artist's initials, as well as the name of the series, the number and the year of the limited edition. Example:

Changes Over Time: The artist has worked with porcelain since 1986. Her work has evolved since then, but she feels that her style has been consistent and recognizably her own throughout.

Doll Sizes: Vera Scholz has crafted 12in (31cm) porcelain babies, but she prefers to work in larger sizes. Many of her child dolls are over a 1m (39in) tall.

Work With Industry: The artist told us that several firms have approached her about manufacturing vinyl dolls from Vera Scholz original designs. As of this writing (May 1992), it is our understanding that the artist has not accepted a contract from any firm with such an interest.

Sale of Molds: "I have sold several dolls to companies which used my originals to craft molds for sale to hobbyists," Vera Scholz said. "With the sole exception of Jan and Julia, made in 1988, all such dolls are smaller than my signed studio originals."

Artist Signature: In 1981 (the year Rotraut began her work as a one-of-a-kind doll artist), she signed her work R1, R2, R3, etc.

From 1982-1986, dolls were signed with the artist's initials, number of the doll and the year. For example: RS-1/82

Beginning in 1987, each Rotraut Schrott original is stamped (see below) and the year when the work was completed is noted.

Since 1985, each Rotraut Schrott original has been accompanied by a certificate.

Work with Industry: "Since 1988, I have worked with the Great American Doll Company (GADCO)," Rotraut said. "From my prototype designs, the firm manufactures limited edition porcelain dolls as well as [unlimited edition] vinyl dolls."

Sale of Molds: "I have sold molds for three prototypes: Martina, Suzi, and Pu Yi. The molds, sold to IMSCO, are each marked 'IMSCO Rotraut Schrott', along with the name of the doll. IMSCO and GADCO are both subsidiaries of AVATAR GENERAL CORPORATION."

Beate Schult

Artist Signature: "From 1974-1984 I made small romantic/nostalgic dolls, each signed on the left hand, with the date and series number," the artist said. "From 1985-1986, my one-of-a-kind leather dolls were signed and dated on the back of the neck."

At the time of our interview, all Beate Schult artist dolls were signed as in (1), below. Her more abstract fantasy *Kunstobjekts* were signed as in (2), below.

(1) **B·S**   (2)

Stylistic Changes over Time: (Refer to text)

Work With Industry: "I have never worked with any commercial firm. My creations are, without exception, products of my own studio," Beate Schult said.

Elfriede Schwarzenbach-Weissenberger

Artist Signature: From 1970-1983, the artist numbered her one-of-a-kind dolls (total of about 200 pieces). Since 1983, dolls are signed at the back of the head under the wig. Signature (see below) includes the artist's initials, E.S., the year and the doll's number within that year.

Changes over Time: Before 1983, hands and feet were fabric stuffed with acrylic. Since 1983, the artist individually sculpts hands and feet for her dolls from wood composition, the same material used for doll heads.

Work With Industry: "No, never!" Elfriede exclaimed.

Sale of Molds: There are no molds. Each doll is handcrafted from start to finish.

Wiltrud Stein

Artist Signature: Wiltrud Stein dolls are signed at the back of the neck. 1983-1985 ceramic dolls are signed as in (1); dolls made in 1985 are signed as in (2). From 1986, dolls bear the artist's full name, date, series number and number within the series (3).

(1)

(2) *Wiltrud*

(3) *Wiltrud Stein 92 91101 – 6/25*

Changes over Time: "From 1983-1985, I worked with clay and only made 2-6 year olds. Features and eyes were painted with acrylic colors," Wiltrud explained. "Since 1985, I have been working with porcelain and craft baby dolls in addition to the older children. From time to time, I change and refine the sculpting of doll hands and feet."

Work with Industry: Beginning in 1991, Wiltrud has worked with SIGIKID®, which manufactures limited-edition vinyl dolls designed after artist-crafted prototypes.

Sale of Molds: "I do not sell my molds," said the artist.

Artist Signature: Vinyl dolls are signed as indicated by (1), below. Porcelain dolls are signed as in (2), with the artist's logo, the number of the series and the doll's name.

(1)

(2)

Name of Doll

Stylistic Changes Over Time: Ruth's earliest dolls were crafted from Cernit®. Since she became a full-time professional doll artist, she has produced studio dolls exclusively in porcelain. Since 1992, she has designed a series of vinyl dolls which are manufactured in a small Spanish factory where work is strictly monitored by the artist.

Work with Industry: Ruth designed her first doll for a commercial doll manufacturer in 1989. In 1992, she began manufacture of her own vinyl series dolls. She continues to craft her porcelain studio dolls at her studio in Wiggensbach in Bavaria.

Sale of Molds: It is our understanding that the artist has not sold any of her doll molds for use by amateurs.

Ingrid Winter ———————————————————

Artist signature: All pieces from this studio are engraved with the artist's name, the name of the doll, the year, and the notation *unikat* (one-of-a-kind). Artist signatures vary; representative samples are reproduced below.

Stylistic changes over time: "My work is constantly changing," Ingrid Winter said, "not because of any commercial motive, but quite simply because repetition bores me." Recently (1992), the artist began to experiment with fixed pose all-porcelain figures, in contrast to her main thrust — posable, porcelain dolls with stuffed fabric bodies and wire armature "skeletons."

Work with Industry: As of 1992, this artist had not elected to work with industry, although she told us she has had various offers of contracts for porcelain and vinyl series dolls.

Sale of Molds: In 1992, the artist planned to begin sale of studio-designed molds. Each mold would be inscribed with the artist's name, the name of the doll, the year, and the name of the manufacturer. As with molds taken from antique dolls, Ingrid Winter molds will produce porcelain doll parts *smaller* than the artist's one-of-a-kind studio originals. She said that the molds would also be less detailed than those she creates for her own artwork.

Artist Signature: "All recent marionettes are signed at the back of the neck with my logo, 'COCO' and the year of production," Claudia Zufferey-Mayer said. "Pieces aren't numbered since I only craft one-of-a-kind figures. Some older work is signed 'C.Mayer' or 'C.Zufferey' or 'CoCo Zu'."

Work with Industry: In 1992, the artist contracted with the German firm, GÖTZ, to design a marionette for the commercial marketplace. The piece is to be offered under the name Coco's Fashion Stage. The artist hopes to develop a series of figures to showcase different stages of 20th century fashion.

Bibliography

In addition to magazine sources from Germany, France and the United States, the authors consulted a number of books while developing their own. Among these are the following, by no means intended as a complete list.

Balanchine, George, *Balanchine's New Complete Stories of The Great Ballets* (Garden City, New York, Doubleday & Company, Inc., 1968)

Braun & Schneider, *Historic Costume in Pictures* (New York, Dover Publications, Inc., 1975) [Reprint of 1905 edition]

Cieslik, Jurgen and Marianne, *Knopf Im Ohr* (Jülich/West Germany, Marianne Cieslik Verlag, 1989)

Cieslik's *Lexikon Der Deutschen Puppenindustrie* (Jülich/ West Germany, Marianne Cieslik Verlag, 1989 edition)

Cieslik's "Puppenmagazin" N°. 1/1987

Conway, Shirley & Wilson, Jean, *100 Years of Steiff, 1880-1980* (Berlin, Ohio, Berlin Printing, 1980)

Forek-Schmahl, Marion, *Directory of Doll Art 1991* (Jülich, Germany, Marianne Cieslik Verlag, 1992)

Forek-Schmahl, Marion, *Kunstobjekt Puppe* (Weingarten, Germany, Kunstverlag Weingarten GmbH, 1990)

Foulke, Jan, 8th, 9th, and 10th *Blue Book of Dolls & Values* (Cumberland, Maryland, Hobby House Press, Inc., 1987, 1989, 1991)

Foulke, Jan, *Focusing on Dolls* (Cumberland, Maryland, Hobby House Press, Inc., 1988)

Gág, Wanda, *More Tales from Grimm* (New York, Coward-McCann, Inc., 1947)

Grimm, J. and W., *German Fairy Tales*, ed. Helmut Brackert and Volkmar Sander (New York, Continuum, 1985)

Hoffman, F.T.A., *The Tales of Hoffman* (New York, The Heritage Press, 1943)

Judd, Polly, *Cloth Dolls of the 1920s and 1930s* (Cumberland, Maryland, Hobby House Press, Inc., 1990)

Lindgren, Astrid, *Ronia, The Robber's Daughter* (New York, The Viking Press, 1983) [Orig. Swedish title: *Ronja Rövardotter* (1981)]

Lister, Margot, *Costume* (Boston, Plays, Inc., 1968)

Mohrenshildt, Annaliese, *Die Kleinen Latscher* (Klagenfurt, Austria, Verlag Carinthia, 1979)

Oroyan, Susanna & Waugh, Carol-Lynn Rössel, *A Collector's Guide to Contemporary Artist Dolls* (Cumberland, Maryland, Hobby House Press, Inc., 1986)

Richter, Joachim F., *Künstler Puppen* (Munich, Lanterna Magica, 1986)

Richter, Joachim F., *Künstler Puppen 2* (Munich, Lanterna Magica, 1989)

Richter, Joachim F., *Künstler Puppen 3* (Munich, Lanterna Magica, 1990)

Richter, Lydia, *The Beloved Käthe Kruse Dolls, Yesterday & Today* (Cumberland, Maryland, Hobby House Press, Inc., 1983)

Riehl, Elli, *Das Kleine Puppenbuch* (Klagenfurt, Austria, Verlag Carinthia, 1978)

Vestner, Heinz (ed.), *Germany* (Signapore, APA Productions (HK) Ltd., *n.d.*)

Wilcox, R. Turner, *The Mode in Costume* (New York, Charles Scribner's Sons, 1958)

Yarwood, Doreen, *The Encyclopedia of World Costume* (New York, Charles Scribner's Sons, 1978)

Notes

Index